Finding Your Lea[...]

As a school leader, do you ever have trouble striking a balance between being agreeable and pleasing your staff, while also being assertive and making the hard decisions? In this empowering new book from Brad Johnson and Jeremy Johnson, you'll discover the tools and insights you need to fine-tune your leadership style and maximize your effectiveness while still building a great culture.

You'll learn how to find the balance between assertiveness and compassion that's right for you, allowing you to address challenges with confidence and empathy. You'll also explore the art of emotional intelligence and its role in building a harmonious school culture, where staff and students thrive. Each chapter is filled with practical strategies and examples to help you build your skills.

As you find your edge as a leader, you'll improve your results for the school and your relationships with staff, and you'll feel more fulfilled in your personal journey as well!

Brad Johnson is one of the most dynamic and engaging speakers in the fields of education and leadership. He has 25 years of experience in the trenches as a teacher and administrator. He is author of many books including *Dear Teacher* (with Hal Bowman), *Principal Bootcamp*, *Putting Teachers First*, and *Learning on Your Feet*. He has travelled the globe speaking and training teachers and educational leaders.

Jeremy Johnson earned a master's degree in Industrial/Organizational Psychology and has 16 years' experience, including a background in administrative processes and procedure development which has led to the implementation of streamlined workflows and improved efficiency in various projects. His exceptional leadership skills have also enabled him to develop and nurture the next generation of leaders within various organizations.

Also available from Brad Johnson & Routledge Eye On Education

www.routledge.com/k-12

Becoming a More Assertive Teacher: Maximizing Strengths, Establishing Boundaries, and Amplifying Your Voice
with Jeremy Johnson

Building Dynamic Teamwork in Schools: 12 Principles of the V Formation to Transform Culture
with Robert Hinchliffe

Dear School Leader: 50 Motivational Quotes and Anecdotes That Affirm Your Purpose and Your Impact

Dear Teacher: 100 Days of Inspirational Quotes and Anecdotes
with Hal Bowman

Thank You, Teacher: 100 Uplifting and Affirming Letters from Your Fellow Educators
with Hal Bowman

Principal Bootcamp: Accelerated Strategies to Influence and Lead from Day One

Putting Teachers First: How to Inspire, Motivate, and Connect with Your Staff

Learning on Your Feet, 2e: Incorporating Physical Activity into the K-8 Classroom
with Melody Jones

What Schools Don't Teach: 20 Ways to Help Students Excel in School and in Life
Brad Johnson and Julie Sessions

From School Administrator to School Leader: 15 Keys to Maximizing Your Leadership Potential
Brad Johnson and Julie Sessions

Finding Your Leadership Edge

Balancing Assertiveness and Compassion in Schools

Brad Johnson and Jeremy Johnson

Routledge
Taylor & Francis Group

NEW YORK AND LONDON

Designed cover image: © Getty Images

First published 2024
by Routledge
605 Third Avenue, New York, NY 10158

and by Routledge
4 Park Square, Milton Park, Abingdon, Oxon, OX14 4RN

Routledge is an imprint of the Taylor & Francis Group, an informa business

© 2024 Brad Johnson and Jeremy Johnson

The right of Brad Johnson and Jeremy Johnson to be identified as authors of this work has been asserted in accordance with sections 77 and 78 of the Copyright, Designs and Patents Act 1988.

Library of Congress Cataloging-in-Publication Data
Names: Johnson, Brad, 1969– author. | Johnson, Jeremy (Psychologist), author.
Title: Finding your leadership edge : balancing assertiveness and
    compassion in schools / Brad Johnson and Jeremy Johnson.
Description: New York, NY : Routledge, 2024. | Series: Routledge eye on
    education | Includes bibliographical references.
Identifiers: LCCN 2023057641 (print) | LCCN 2023057642 (ebook) |
    ISBN 9781032657738 (hardback) | ISBN 9781032644073 (paperback) |
    ISBN 9781032657745 (ebook)
Subjects: LCSH: School administrators—Professional relationships. |
    School principals—Professional relationships. | Educational leadership. |
    School management and organization. | School environment.
Classification: LCC LB2831.8 .J65 2024 (print) | LCC LB2831.8 (ebook) |
    DDC 371.2/011—dc23/eng/20240131
LC record available at https://lccn.loc.gov/2023057641
LC ebook record available at https://lccn.loc.gov/2023057642

ISBN: 978-1-032-65773-8 (hbk)
ISBN: 978-1-032-64407-3 (pbk)
ISBN: 978-1-032-65774-5 (ebk)

DOI: 10.4324/9781032657745

Typeset in Palatino
by Apex CoVantage, LLC

Contents

Reflection Quizzes

Welcome to our Reflection Quizzes, which are primarily intended to introduce you to and familiarize you with three essential leadership concepts: compassion, assertiveness, and agreeableness. These quizzes are purely informational, designed to provide you with an overview of the different ranges within these facets of leadership. Remember that there is no one-size-fits-all approach to leadership, and these quizzes are here to give you a better understanding of the various aspects within these concepts.

Each leadership style has its strengths and may be more effective in specific situations. No one side of the spectrum is inherently better than the other, and understanding your own tendencies can guide your growth as a leader. So, take these quizzes with an open mind and an eagerness to learn more about yourself and your leadership potential.

DOI: 10.4324/9781032657745-1

Main Reflection Quiz 1

1. I am generally caring towards others who are struggling.

1	2	3	4	5
Strongly Disagree	Disagree	Neutral	Agree	Strongly Agree

2. I find that I tend to pay extra attention when someone is sharing their issues with me.

1	2	3	4	5
Strongly Disagree	Disagree	Neutral	Agree	Strongly Agree

3. I regularly find myself comforting or aiding those who are stressed or depressed.

1	2	3	4	5
Strongly Disagree	Disagree	Neutral	Agree	Strongly Agree

4. Even though I may not always see eye to eye with others, I understand that as individuals, we all share common difficulties.

1	2	3	4	5
Strongly Disagree	Disagree	Neutral	Agree	Strongly Agree

5. I can tell when there is something bothering someone without being told.

1	2	3	4	5
Strongly Disagree	Disagree	Neutral	Agree	Strongly Agree

6. I have regularly been told that I am a good listener.

1	2	3	4	5
Strongly Disagree	Disagree	Neutral	Agree	Strongly Agree

7. I make it a priority to be there for others who are experiencing difficult situations.

1	2	3	4	5
Strongly Disagree	Disagree	Neutral	Agree	Strongly Agree

8. I am drawn to those who are experiencing difficulties.

1	2	3	4	5
Strongly Disagree	Disagree	Neutral	Agree	Strongly Agree

9. I regularly think about how I can help others with their issues.

1	2	3	4	5
Strongly Disagree	Disagree	Neutral	Agree	Strongly Agree

10. I think that it's important to realize that we all have weaknesses, and that is one of the reasons that relationships are important.

1	2	3	4	5
Strongly Disagree	Disagree	Neutral	Agree	Strongly Agree

11. I feel like I tune-in rather than tune-out when individuals start sharing personal problems.

1	2	3	4	5
Strongly Disagree	Disagree	Neutral	Agree	Strongly Agree

12. I feel emotionally connected to people who are distressed.

1	2	3	4	5
Strongly Disagree	Disagree	Neutral	Agree	Strongly Agree

Score: _____

Remember, this is a facet of leadership behavior, and no one side of the spectrum is better than another. Certain traits are more effective for certain tasks.

12–28   Leaders with low compassion struggle to understand and connect with their team's emotions, often appearing indifferent or uncaring. They provide minimal emotional support and may prioritize tasks over well-being, resulting in a less supportive and connected team.

29–44 Leaders with moderate compassion can grasp their team's feelings to some extent and provide occasional support. They aim for a balance between tasks and well-being, but the level of support may vary. Team morale may fluctuate based on the situation.

45–60 Leaders with high compassion deeply understand and genuinely care about their team's emotions and well-being. They consistently offer emotional support, prioritize both tasks and team welfare, and foster a positive, supportive work environment with high team morale, where members feel valued and motivated.

Main Reflection Quiz 2

1. I have no issue dealing with difficult situations involving confrontation.

1	2	3	4	5
Strongly Disagree	Disagree	Neutral	Agree	Strongly Agree

2. I express my opinions, even if others in the group disagree with me.

1	2	3	4	5
Strongly Disagree	Disagree	Neutral	Agree	Strongly Agree

3. I have no problem refusing requests from others.

1	2	3	4	5
Strongly Disagree	Disagree	Neutral	Agree	Strongly Agree

4. I feel comfortable saying no to people.

1	2	3	4	5
Strongly Disagree	Disagree	Neutral	Agree	Strongly Agree

5. I am comfortable stepping in and making decisions for others.

1	2	3	4	5
Strongly Disagree	Disagree	Neutral	Agree	Strongly Agree

6. I speak clearly, concisely, and address situations directly.

1	2	3	4	5
Strongly Disagree	Disagree	Neutral	Agree	Strongly Agree

7. I have a difficult time compromising my needs, wants, or goals.

1	2	3	4	5
Strongly Disagree	Disagree	Neutral	Agree	Strongly Agree

8. I speak up when someone is not respecting my personal boundaries.

1	2	3	4	5
Strongly Disagree	Disagree	Neutral	Agree	Strongly Agree

9. I do not find it difficult to ask tough questions or present opposing viewpoints to other's ideas.

1	2	3	4	5
Strongly Disagree	Disagree	Neutral	Agree	Strongly Agree

10. I frequently know exactly what I want and how to get it.

1	2	3	4	5
Strongly Disagree	Disagree	Neutral	Agree	Strongly Agree

11. I regularly direct the flow of conversations and/or meetings.

1	2	3	4	5
Strongly Disagree	Disagree	Neutral	Agree	Strongly Agree

12. I feel like I push boundaries at times, but I also try to make it right.

1	2	3	4	5
Strongly Disagree	Disagree	Neutral	Agree	Strongly Agree

Score: _____

Remember, this is a facet of leadership behavior, and no one side of the spectrum is better than another. Certain traits are more effective for certain tasks.

12–28 Leaders with low assertiveness tend to be passive in their communication, hesitating to express their thoughts and avoiding difficult conversations. They struggle with decision-making, often deferring to others or avoiding decisions altogether. Conflict resolution is a challenge, as they tend to avoid addressing issues, allowing problems to persist.

29–44 Leaders with medium assertiveness strike a balance between passive and aggressive communication. They can express their thoughts but may not always do so assertively. They make decisions, but not consistently, and may seek consensus rather than taking charge. Conflict resolution is addressed as needed but may lack assertiveness in achieving swift resolutions.

45–60 Leaders with high assertiveness are confident and direct in their communication, expressing themselves clearly and respectfully. They take charge in decision-making, are proactive in guiding their team, and make tough decisions when required. Conflict is addressed promptly and assertively, with a problem-solving approach that facilitates productive resolution.

Additional Reflection Quiz

1. I often go out of my way to help others, even if it means sacrificing my own time and resources.

1	2	3	4	5
Strongly Disagree	Disagree	Neutral	Agree	Strongly Agree

2. I am comfortable with compromising when resolving conflicts and disputes.

1	2	3	4	5
Strongly Disagree	Disagree	Neutral	Agree	Strongly Agree

3. I find it difficult to say no when someone asks me to take on extra work or responsibilities.

1	2	3	4	5
Strongly Disagree	Disagree	Neutral	Agree	Strongly Agree

4. I prefer to avoid conflicts and disagreements at work.

1	2	3	4	5
Strongly Disagree	Disagree	Neutral	Agree	Strongly Agree

5. I tend to be indirect in dealing with issues with others.

1	2	3	4	5
Strongly Disagree	Disagree	Neutral	Agree	Strongly Agree

6. I am typically very easy to satisfy.

1	2	3	4	5
Strongly Disagree	Disagree	Neutral	Agree	Strongly Agree

Score: _____

Remember, this is a facet of personality, and no one side of the spectrum is better than another. Certain traits are more effective for certain tasks.

6–17   Leaders with low agreeableness prioritize their goals over others, making assertive decisions even if it leads to conflict. They are direct in addressing conflicts and may focus more on tasks than relationships.

18–30   Leaders with high agreeableness prioritize harmony and relationships, often involving team members in decision-making and resolving conflicts through compromise. They create a supportive and inclusive work environment and excel in interpersonal relationships.

1

Discovering Your Leadership Edge

Amidst the thundering roar of Niagara Falls, a world-class tight-rope walker stepped onto a slender rope, suspended high above the churning waters. As he embarked on this daring feat, a vast crowd gathered, their collective breath held in awe and anticipation. This heart-stopping spectacle, much like the journey of being a school leader, demanded a unique set of skills, the willingness to put oneself out there, and the ability to find balance in the face of adversity. The story of Charles Blondin's daring tightrope walk across Niagara Falls serves as a powerful reminder that the balancing act of assertiveness and compassion is not a dilemma but a source of unparalleled strength for educational leaders.

Just as Blondin faced the daunting challenge of that narrow rope suspended high above the falls, educational leaders find themselves navigating a perilous path, high above the diverse demands and aspirations of their stakeholders. Like the crowd that gathered to witness Blondin's feat, educational leaders encounter a spectrum of perspectives – some critical, some supportive, and some merely observing. It mirrors the complex landscape they must navigate.

Blondin's initial wobbles on the rope symbolize the uncertainty and pressure that educational leaders may feel when striving to harmonize the expectations of innovation and tradition. As Blondin demonstrated, determination and skill can ultimately win trust and admiration. His ability to walk without

DOI: 10.4324/9781032657745-2

a balancing pole, sit on a chair, juggle, and even make lunch on the rope showcases the rewards for educational leaders who find the right balance between innovation and tradition, earning the respect and support of their stakeholders.

The pivotal moment comes when Blondin asks for a volunteer to ride in a wheelbarrow across Niagara Falls. Even though they had seen all his incredible feats, no one would get into the wheelbarrow, not one single person. However, the story goes that there was one person who was willing to be carried across by Blondin, and that was his manager, who not only believed in his competence but had a relationship with him. Since there was a history of trust in their relationship, he was willing to take the risk. This underscores the critical role of trust in leadership.

In this context, the delicate balance between assertiveness and compassion becomes the linchpin of success for educational leaders. Assertiveness, like Blondin's confident steps on the tightrope, is necessary for conveying a clear vision, setting high standards, and driving innovation. However, compassion, akin to the trust Blondin's manager had in him, is indispensable for building relationships, understanding stakeholders' needs, and nurturing a supportive environment.

Just as Blondin's manager entrusted him with his life, educational leaders need the trust and support of their stakeholders to bring their educational visions to life. They must boldly step onto the tightrope of leadership, skillfully balancing assertiveness and compassion, and in doing so, they gain an edge that propels them towards unparalleled effectiveness in their roles. Like Blondin, they inspire awe and admiration as they lead their schools to success, one courageous step at a time.

Building Trust Capital

The trust exhibited by Blondin's manager is the kind of trust that a school leader desires to have in their staff. Not someone who just thinks they're great, but someone willing to get into the wheelbarrow with them because they trust them. This is where the importance of building trust with your staff comes into play.

Trust capital is akin to investing in a savings account, where educational leaders deposit the currency of trust through their actions and interactions. It serves as the foundation for nurturing deep, caring relationships among staff, creating an environment of camaraderie and mutual respect within the educational institution.

Just as you deposit money into a savings account for future use, trust capital is built through the ongoing deposits of respect, understanding, and support. These deposits are made by educational leaders who take the time to comprehend each staff member's aspirations and challenges, recognizing their individuality and the diverse facets of their lives. In this analogy, understanding the staff's unique needs and goals is akin to putting money into the trust account, an investment that can be withdrawn when needed.

Trust capital is not a one-way transaction but a mutual endeavor. It involves both leaders and staff working collaboratively to build this reserve of trust. Educational leaders place significant value on staff feedback, actively incorporating it into the decision-making processes of the institution. This participation and inclusion is equivalent to additional deposits into the trust account, growing the capital of trust that can be drawn upon when challenges arise or when support and unity are required.

In essence, trust capital acts as a financial safeguard, an account filled with goodwill and faith cultivated over time through consistent, reliable, and transparent interactions. Just as you might rely on your savings when unexpected expenses arise, educational leaders and staff draw from this trust capital during times of adversity, maintaining the strength of the school community and preserving unity.

Trust in Leadership: The Charles Blondin Analogy

Educational leaders, much like the renowned tightrope walker Charles Blondin, find themselves navigating a high wire act, suspended above the tumultuous waters of diverse stakeholder demands. In this perilous journey, they are tasked with the challenging mission of striking a delicate balance between innovation and tradition. In this quest, the importance of trust cannot be overstated. Trust forms the bedrock upon which educational leaders can secure the vital support of their stakeholders, especially when it comes to introducing innovative educational initiatives.

The tightrope analogy serves as a powerful reminder of the intricate dance between assertiveness and compassion that educational leaders must perform. On one hand, assertiveness is a necessary tool for conveying a clear and unwavering vision. It's about setting high standards and fostering innovation by confidently articulating the path forward. However, assertiveness alone can be cold and unyielding. This is where compassion steps in, providing the warmth and understanding that is essential for building relationships and nurturing a supportive environment.

The skillful educational leader knows when to be firm in their decisions, employing assertiveness to maintain direction and resolve, much like Blondin's unwavering steps on the narrow rope. It's about establishing a sense of purpose and direction within the school community, setting expectations that drive progress and growth.

Simultaneously, compassion, akin to the trust Blondin's manager had in him, plays a pivotal role in establishing a nurturing and empathetic atmosphere. It's indispensable for understanding the needs and concerns of the stakeholders, which include teachers, students, and parents. Compassion nurtures relationships, fosters an inclusive environment, and communicates that everyone's voices and needs are valued.

Just as Blondin's manager entrusted him with his life, educational leaders need the trust and support of their stakeholders to bring their educational visions to life. They must boldly step onto the tightrope of leadership, skillfully balancing assertiveness and compassion. In doing so, they gain an edge that propels them towards unparalleled effectiveness in their roles. Much like Blondin who inspired awe and admiration, as they lead their school to success one courageous step at a time, educational leaders inspire those around them with a harmonious blend of assertiveness and compassion.

Building Trust with Teachers and Staff

To build trust, leaders must create a supportive and inclusive environment, akin to a nurturing ecosystem that thrives on respect and understanding. Acknowledging and appreciating the relentless efforts of the staff is a vital aspect of leadership. It not only signifies respect for their hard work but also showcases the leader's compassion for their well-being and contributions.

The compassionate leader extends their care beyond the confines of the office, into the daily interactions and shared spaces where informal conversations and bonding occur. Small talk, inquiries about personal lives, and a genuine interest in the well-being of each staff member create a sense of camaraderie and trust, much like investing in the emotional capital of the team.

Transparency is the cornerstone of trust-building. Leaders who communicate openly and honestly create an environment where individuals feel secure. This openness extends to sharing the school's vision, goals, and challenges. When everyone is on the same page, it leads to a shared understanding that is vital for unity and trust.

However, building trust with teachers and staff is not merely a one-way street but a mutual effort. Involving teachers in decision-making processes empowers them and sends a clear message that their input holds weight. It's not just about token participation but a genuine desire to consider their insights and input when shaping policies and practices. This involvement strengthens the bonds of trust, as it communicates that their perspectives truly matter and are integral to the school's success.

Leader, not Administrator: Shifting the Paradigm in Education

To build a culture of trust, we need people who are effective leaders and not just administrators. We seem to have people who are more comfortable in the role of an administrator than that of a true leader. This underscores a systemic issue tied to how we prepare individuals for leadership roles in education. Unfortunately, despite efforts to adapt to 21st-century learning, leadership practices have remained largely unchanged since the industrial revolution. In essence, educational leadership was initially built on a transactional foundation of rewards and punishments – that emerged during the industrial revolution and forms the basis for numerous management and administrative concepts.

Given that leadership profoundly influences school culture, motivation, morale, and overall functioning, the persistence of this traditional approach may contribute to many of the challenges seen in education today, such as low teacher morale and a high turnover rate among principals. Interestingly, it's the transactional leadership style that prevails as the most used approach. This style involves setting objectives and goals for followers and relies on rewards and punishments to ensure compliance with these objectives. Unfortunately, it's also the least effective leadership style, even though it closely aligns with administrative responsibilities.

When we think of leaders who haven't been effective in their roles (and we've all encountered them at some point), they often exhibit a compliance-based style of leadership. This tendency toward compliance can be traced back to their traditional training. Notably, many educational programs are labeled as "education administration" rather than "leadership," reinforcing the transactional approach. This isn't to condemn transactional leadership outright, but it's crucial to recognize that its primary focus on control, organization, and short-term planning falls short of fully unleashing the potential of leaders and their followers.

This style may produce short-term results, especially in straightforward situations where a system of rewards and punishments effectively motivates followers. However, it conspicuously lacks the capacity to stimulate innovation, foster creativity, or facilitate long-term planning that requires input from staff. Additionally, it's important to acknowledge that in the educational context, the pressure to implement quick changes – such as raising test scores – often pushes principals toward transactional leadership. Unfortunately, this leaves little room for principals to evolve into effective leaders. Leaders can't solely rely on transactional approaches to create a positive culture within their staff. While it's true that not all transactional leaders are inherently ineffective, this style's reliance on compliance often results in a less productive and less effective leadership dynamic. A defining characteristic of this approach is typically, "do as I say, not as I do."

In essence, it's crucial that we reevaluate our approaches to leadership in the education sector. Transactional leadership, while having its merits in certain contexts, must be complemented by more adaptive, transformative, and visionary leadership styles that better align with the ever-evolving demands and complexities of modern education. The path to effective leadership in education requires a shift from mere administration to genuine leadership – a journey with the potential to create a more positive, dynamic, and effective educational landscape for all stakeholders involved.

It's evident that a recalibration of our approach to leadership within the education sector is long overdue. Our traditional methods must be supplemented by more adaptive, transformative, and visionary leadership styles that better align with the evolving demands and complexities of modern education. We need a more balanced approach to leadership to be most effective, and this is where the art of balancing assertiveness and compassion complements that need perfectly.

Achieving this balance can help education leaders move beyond mere administration by nurturing a positive culture, fostering innovation, and inspiring lasting change within their educational institutions. By embracing a leadership style that values collaboration, empowers educators, and prioritizes the well-being of all stakeholders, we can pave the way for a brighter future in education, one where true leadership takes center stage, and positive outcomes for students and staff become the norm.

Leadership Edge: Authenticity and Impact

Think of the concept of a leadership edge as your guiding compass, pointing educational leaders towards authentic and profoundly impactful leadership. It serves as the unique blend of your skills, qualities, and experiences that distinguishes you as a leader. Your leadership edge is the intersection of your strengths, values, and passions, shaping a distinct leadership style that mirrors your true self.

Uncovering and harnessing your leadership edge goes beyond mere differentiation; it's about leading with unwavering authenticity and making an enduring impact on the lives of those you lead. It's about becoming a leader who leaves an indelible mark on your school community, inspiring others to reach their full potential.

Your leadership edge isn't just about mastering leadership; it's equally about mastering the art of understanding the individuals you lead. It involves comprehending the unique needs, aspirations, and challenges of your staff and students. It's the skill to tailor your leadership style to resonate with the individuals and groups under your guidance.

This delicate balance encompasses not only what you know as a leader but also delves deeply into the realm of understanding your team. It's recognizing that leadership isn't a one-way street; it's a dynamic exchange where your knowledge converges with the needs and dreams of your team. This equilibrium fuels effective leadership, where you apply your expertise while also being an attentive listener, a perpetual learner, and an agile responder to the evolving needs of your staff.

Furthermore, it's about rallying everyone on board with a shared mission or vision. Your leadership edge includes the ability to articulate a compelling vision that captivates your team, uniting them in pursuit of a common objective. It's about nurturing a sense of belonging and dedication, where all stakeholders feel an unwavering connection to the mission and are galvanized to work collectively in its realization.

Your leadership edge is not a one-size-fits-all blueprint; it is as unique as your fingerprint. It defines how you inspire and motivate your team, how you navigate challenges and resolve conflicts, and how you embrace change and uncertainty as opportunities for growth. When you tap into your leadership edge, you create a transformative school culture, empowering both your staff and students to thrive.

To uncover your leadership edge, embark on a journey of self-reflection and self-awareness. Explore your core values, explore your singular strengths, and contemplate the impact you aspire to create as a leader. Ponder the invaluable lessons garnered from your life's experiences, including both the triumphs and the trials. By intimately comprehending yourself and those you lead, you can excavate your leadership edge and employ it as your guiding compass, shaping your choices and actions in a manner that aligns seamlessly with your authentic leadership style.

Developing your Leadership Edge

Developing your leadership edge is not just about gaining knowledge; it's about embarking on a transformative journey of self-discovery and growth as a leader. As you read the chapters of this book, you're not merely absorbing insights into leadership concepts; you're on a quest to unlock your true leadership potential. Each chapter serves as a stepping stone on this path, offering a wealth of wisdom and practical guidance to empower you.

The lessons shared in these chapters are not confined to theory; they are actionable, providing you with the tools and strategies necessary to not only deepen your understanding of leadership but also to implement positive changes within your school community. By embracing the concepts presented and engaging with the practical exercises, you are not simply enhancing your leadership skills – you are igniting a profound transformation within your school, your team, and the lives of the students you serve.

As you embark on this reading journey, prepare yourself not only to expand your knowledge but also to evolve as a leader. You will uncover facets of your leadership style and even your strengths that you may not have realized existed, and you will learn how to harness them for the greater good of your school community.

Once you've discovered your leadership edge, the journey continues with the vital task of developing and refining your leadership skills. Leadership is not a static concept; it's dynamic and adaptable, and your skills can be cultivated and honed through intentional practice and self-improvement.

Here are some powerful strategies to aid you on your path to leadership development:

- ◆ **Identify strengths:** Identifying your strengths is the foundational step in your journey towards effective leadership. Self-awareness and feedback from others play a crucial role in this process. Begin with a thorough self-assessment, reflecting on your past experiences and recognizing patterns of success. Ask yourself what skills or qualities consistently stood out in these situations. Additionally, don't hesitate to seek input from colleagues, mentors, and those who know you well. Their perspectives can provide valuable insights and complement your self-assessment.

- ◆ **Leverage strengths:** Once you've identified your strengths, the next critical phase is leveraging them strategically in your leadership approach. This involves recognizing opportunities where your unique abilities can be most impactful within your school community. Define clear objectives for how you intend to use your strengths and create action plans that outline the steps required for implementation. Collaborate with your team and colleagues to integrate your strengths into group initiatives, fostering a culture of cooperation and shared success.

- ◆ **Focus on continuous improvement** is key in this process. Regularly assess the impact of leveraging your strengths and adjust your approach based on feedback and results. Your ability to inspire others by exemplifying the effective use of strengths can also motivate your team members to identify and apply their own unique qualities. As you incorporate your strengths into your leadership style, you'll not only become a more authentic and influential leader but also contribute significantly to the positive growth and development of your school community.

- ◆ **Seek mentorship:** Finding a mentor can be a transformative step in your leadership journey. A mentor is like a seasoned guide who can illuminate the path ahead. They possess a wealth of knowledge and experience that they willingly share with you. Their insights are like gems, helping you navigate complex leadership challenges with more clarity and confidence. A mentor provides constructive feedback, offering you a mirror through which you can assess your leadership style objectively. Their stories and experiences become a rich source of inspiration, showcasing both successes and setbacks, which are invaluable lessons. Through this mentorship, you not only gain wisdom but also develop a deeper understanding of yourself as a leader, refining your leadership edge.

◆ **Read leadership literature:** Immerse yourself in the world of leadership literature, where you'll discover a vast repository of wisdom waiting to be explored. Books and articles penned by renowned leadership experts offer fresh perspectives and actionable ideas. These readings serve as windows into different leadership philosophies and strategies. They challenge your thinking, encouraging you to question the status quo and seek innovative approaches. Each page turned is an opportunity to expand your leadership horizons and gather valuable tools for your leadership toolkit. It's a continuous journey of self-improvement through the insights of those who have walked the leadership path before you.

◆ **Join professional networks:** Becoming a part of professional networks or associations is akin to joining a community of like-minded individuals who share your passion for growth and excellence in educational leadership. These networks offer a platform for collaboration, learning, and sharing best practices. Through engaging with your peers in the field, you gain fresh perspectives, learn from their experiences, and exchange valuable insights. Professional networks also provide a sense of belonging, where you realize that you're not alone on your leadership journey. You can seek advice, participate in discussions, and draw inspiration from the collective wisdom of your fellow leaders.

♦ **Attend leadership workshops and seminars**: Leadership is a dynamic and evolving skill, and attending workshops and seminars is an excellent way to stay updated and enhance your competencies. These events provide structured learning environments where you can focus on specific leadership skills or areas of development. They offer hands-on experiences and interactive sessions that allow you to practice and refine your leadership techniques. Furthermore, these gatherings often bring together leaders who are equally eager to learn and grow. The connections you form in these settings can become valuable sources of support and collaboration in your leadership endeavors.

♦ **Practice self-reflection:** Self-reflection is the compass that helps you navigate your leadership journey. Regularly setting aside time for self-reflection allows you to pause, step back, and assess your leadership practices. It's a moment to ponder what strategies are yielding positive results and which areas might need improvement. Self-reflection fosters a deep awareness of your leadership style and its impact on your school community. It's a tool for continuous improvement, enabling you to align your leadership with your leadership edge. Through self-reflection, you not only learn from your experiences but also gain a deeper understanding of the path you want to chart as a leader.

Remember, developing your leadership skills is an ongoing journey, not a destination. Be proactive in your pursuit of growth, remain open to feedback, and embrace new perspectives. The more you invest in your development, the more profound and impactful your leadership will become. It's a journey that holds the power to transform not only your leadership style but the entire educational landscape you serve.

2

Understanding Agreeableness

A Key to Effective
Teacher–Leader Relationships

Assertiveness is a set of communication and behavioral skills that revolve around expressing one's thoughts, feelings, and needs directly and respectfully, all while respecting the rights and boundaries of others. It involves confidently and effectively communicating your opinions, desires, and boundaries without resorting to aggression or passivity. This skill is crucial for maintaining order and communication within any organization, including a school. By using assertiveness, educational leaders can effectively communicate expectations, make important decisions, and address issues promptly and directly. This approach creates a sense of structure and accountability among teachers and staff, ensuring that everyone is on the same page.

However, assertiveness alone is not enough. Compassion plays an equally significant role when dealing with teachers, who often value harmonious relationships and may be sensitive to conflicts or criticism. Teaching tends to attract individuals with high levels of agreeableness due to the field's emphasis on interpersonal skills. Many teachers are naturally empathetic, caring, and oriented towards others, making compassion an essential trait for school leaders. Compassion enables educational leaders to recognize

DOI: 10.4324/9781032657745-3

the challenges and pressures that teachers may face. By showing empathy and understanding, leaders foster trust and open communication. When teachers feel heard, supported, and valued, they are more likely to be motivated and engaged in their work.

Striking a balance between assertiveness and compassion is key to creating a school culture that promotes both accountability and emotional well-being. Assertiveness ensures that expectations are clear and consistently upheld, while compassion acknowledges the individual needs and experiences of teachers. This approach fosters a positive and collaborative work environment, enhancing job satisfaction and promoting a sense of belonging among staff. School leaders play a vital role in supporting and empowering their teachers, and finding the right balance between assertiveness and compassion is essential for creating an environment where teachers can thrive and contribute their best to the success of the school community.

Now, let's shift our focus to the leadership exemplified by Gene Kranz in the movie *Apollo 13*. Gene Kranz served as the mission control leader during a critical space mission when an oxygen tank exploded on the spacecraft, putting the lives of astronauts in immediate danger. In this high-stakes situation, Kranz embodies balanced leadership by effectively combining assertiveness with agreeableness. His assertiveness is evident in his unwavering determination to solve complex problems and overcome obstacles faced by the astronauts. He takes charge and quickly establishes control over the mission control room, ensuring that every decision made is in the best interest of the astronauts and their safe return.

However, Gene Kranz's leadership style goes beyond assertiveness. He also demonstrates a remarkable level of agreeableness, particularly in his interactions with his team of engineers and experts. Kranz recognizes the importance of teamwork and fosters an atmosphere of collaboration and mutual respect. Instead of dictating orders, he actively seeks input from his team members, valuing their expertise and encouraging open communication. This agreeableness allows diverse perspectives and innovative solutions to emerge, significantly enhancing the chances of a successful rescue mission.

The profound moral lesson in Kranz's balanced leadership approach in the face of a crisis is that it highlights the significance of maintaining control and making tough decisions while simultaneously fostering a collaborative and supportive environment. By combining assertiveness with agreeableness, he creates a sense of unity and shared purpose among the mission control team, fostering trust and cooperation even in the most challenging circumstances. Kranz's leadership in *Apollo 13* serves as an inspiring example of how balanced leadership can lead to remarkable achievements, emphasizing the value of assertiveness and compassion in leadership roles.

What Is Agreeableness?

Agreeableness is a personality trait that encompasses an individual's inclination towards cooperation, compassion, and consideration for others. As one of the widely recognized Big Five personality traits, it holds significant importance in psychological studies. It is important to note that agreeableness is not inherently positive or negative, as it encompasses a diverse range of behaviors and attitudes. Those with high levels of agreeableness often exhibit traits such as empathy, kindness, and a desire for harmonious relationships. On the other hand, individuals with lower levels of agreeableness may be more direct, independent, and a focus on their own needs.

Having high or low levels of agreeableness has its pros and cons, depending on the situation. If you're high in agreeableness, you're great at teamwork and getting along with others, but you might find it hard to stand up for yourself, or you might be easily influenced. On the other hand, if you're low in agreeableness, you're more direct and independent in your thinking, which can be an advantage, but it might strain your relationships and lead to conflicts. The key is to recognize that agreeableness can be valuable in different circumstances and personal goals. It's important to note that neither high nor low agreeableness means you're naturally assertive. Being assertive requires intentional effort and skill-building. So, whether you scored high or low on the agreeableness quiz, remember that if you want to be more assertive, it's something you'll need to work on.

As a leader, it is also important to understand that you lead a staff of people who may also score high or low in agreeableness. For instance, have you ever wondered why you have some teachers who are highly empathetic, rarely speak up for themselves, or have trouble saying no, yet have some teachers who have no problem saying no, and are highly competitive or easily advocate for themselves? These are all traits from either end of the agreeableness spectrum. The personality trait of agreeableness is one of the five major dimensions of personality known as the Big Five traits. Agreeableness refers to an individual's tendency to be cooperative, compassionate, considerate, and friendly in their interactions with others. People who score high on agreeableness are generally warm-hearted, empathetic, and concerned about the well-being of others. On the other hand, those who score low on agreeableness may be more competitive, assertive, and focused on their own interests.

It is important to understand the impact of agreeableness on your leadership style and the dynamics within your school community. Agreeableness, as a personality trait, influences how we interact with others, make decisions, and foster relationships. In this chapter, we will explore the importance of understanding high and low agreeableness for leaders, highlighting five positive and five negative attributes associated with each so you can become more self-aware as a leader. Understand that while you can't really change your personality trait of agreeableness, since it is considered to be relatively stable over time, you can become more aware of the advantages and disadvantages based upon your assessment that you took at the beginning of the book. And you can also build your assertive skill set to balance the areas in which you lack certain skills, so that you can express your thoughts, feelings, opinions, needs, and boundaries directly and respectfully.

High Agreeableness: Advantages

If you are a high-agreeableness leader, you possess a unique set of qualities that contribute to your exceptional leadership style.

Your approach is centered on collaboration, empathy, openness to diverse perspectives, and the cultivation of strong relationships. These traits are the building blocks of a positive and inclusive school environment where everyone feels valued and supported.

You prioritize collaboration and teamwork, valuing collective input and fostering a sense of ownership among stakeholders. You actively involve teachers, students, parents, and staff members in decision-making processes. For example, when planning a new school initiative, you may organize a collaborative team consisting of teachers, parents, and administrators to gather diverse perspectives and ensure everyone's voice is heard.

Your high degree of empathy and compassion enables you to understand the needs and emotions of staff, students, and parents. You demonstrate genuine care, provide support, and create a nurturing environment where individuals feel understood and valued. For instance, if a teacher is going through a personal hardship, you would take the time to listen, offer understanding, and provide resources or accommodations to alleviate their burden. Your empathy helps create a culture of support and well-being within the school community.

You are open to diverse perspectives and value the input of others. You create an atmosphere where individuals feel comfortable expressing their opinions, fostering a culture of trust, respect, and open communication. You encourage teachers, staff, and parents to share their ideas, concerns, and suggestions without fear of judgment. By actively seeking and considering different viewpoints, you create a vibrant and inclusive environment where everyone's contributions are valued.

You invest time and effort in building strong relationships with staff, students, and parents. You actively engage with individuals, show appreciation, and create a sense of belonging within the school community. You make an effort to get to know your staff, students, and parents individually, showing genuine interest and care. You actively participate in conversations, attend school events, and recognize and appreciate the efforts of those around you. By fostering positive relationships, you create a supportive and collaborative environment that enhances the overall school experience for everyone involved.

Approachability is a key trait exhibited by agreeable leaders, and it plays a vital role in fostering a positive and inclusive school environment. Leaders who are approachable are not only accessible to students, staff, and parents but also create a welcoming atmosphere where individuals feel comfortable reaching out for support, guidance, or to share their thoughts and concerns.

You are a leader who understands the power of collaboration, empathy, openness, and relationship-building. By actively involving stakeholders in decision-making, demonstrating empathy and compassion, valuing diverse perspectives, and investing in strong relationships, you create an environment where everyone feels heard, understood, and appreciated.

High Agreeableness: Disadvantages

Being a high-agreeableness leader comes with its own set of challenges. The tendency to prioritize maintaining positive relationships and avoiding conflict can hinder your ability to make tough decisions that are in the best interest of the school. While high agreeableness can be advantageous, it is important to recognize negative attributes that may arise.

As a high-agreeableness leader, you may prioritize maintaining positive relationships and avoiding conflict over making tough decisions. They may tend to prioritize harmony over merit, overlooking or downplaying the importance of objective evaluation. This can result in compromised standards, favoritism, and a lack of accountability within the school. It is crucial for leaders to find a balance between maintaining relationships and making decisions based on merit. For example, let's say there is a teacher who consistently underperforms and fails to meet the required standards of instruction. Despite recognizing the issue, the agreeable leader may hesitate to address the problem directly with the teacher, fearing that it will strain their relationship or cause conflict. As a result, the teacher's inadequate performance continues to impact student learning and the overall quality of education provided.

Due to their desire to please others, agreeable leaders may avoid addressing performance issues directly. Difficult conversations about performance or delivering unfavorable news may be delayed or altogether avoided. However, this approach hinders the resolution of problems and impedes the overall growth of the school. Leaders must learn to address performance issues promptly and constructively to ensure a positive learning environment for all.

While seeking consensus is valuable and fosters a sense of collaboration, high-agreeableness leaders may overly prioritize consensus-building and delay decision-making processes. This can hinder progress and prevent timely responses to challenges or opportunities. It is important for leaders to strike a balance between seeking consensus and making timely decisions.

Another challenge faced by high-agreeableness leaders is their inability to say "no" to requests or demands, even when they are unreasonable or not in the best interest of the school. This can lead to overcommitment, stretched resources, and an inability to prioritize effectively. Leaders must learn to set boundaries and communicate their limitations assertively, understanding that saying "no" when necessary is essential for maintaining their own well-being and ensuring the success of the school.

Because agreeable leaders value harmonious relationships, you may be more vulnerable to manipulation or influence from others who may have personal agendas. This can result in compromised decision-making, favoritism, and the exploitation of your agreeable nature.

Your ability to make tough decisions while maintaining positive relationships is a valuable skill. By navigating these challenges with awareness and assertiveness, you can create an environment that fosters growth, accountability, and student success.

Low Agreeableness: Advantages

If you are low agreeableness then you exhibit independent thinking, direct communication, boundary setting, and a results-oriented approach. By embodying these traits, you bring a unique perspective to the school and foster an environment conducive to growth and success. Here is how these traits can contribute positively to your leadership style.

One of the most common traits is assertiveness in decision-making. You possess the confidence to express your opinions and are less swayed by external influences. This assertiveness allows you to make choices that align with your vision for the school and the goals you have set. By remaining resolute and determined, you can lead their staff, students, and the entire school community towards a clear and defined path of progress.

You have the ability to challenge the status quo and explore alternative approaches. You embrace innovation and fresh perspectives, recognizing that they can lead to positive change within the school community. By encouraging independent thinking and being unafraid to take calculated risks, you can inspire creativity and foster a culture of growth among your staff and students.

Your direct communication style is one of your strengths. By prioritizing clarity and transparency, you ensure that your messages are effectively conveyed and understood by staff, students, and parents. Your straightforward and concise approach promotes efficiency, prevents misunderstandings, and facilitates timely decision-making. Through direct communication, you build trust and cultivate a positive and open culture within your school.

Maintaining a healthy work–life balance is essential for any leader, and as a low-agreeableness leader, you excel at setting and maintaining boundaries. You understand the importance of prioritizing your well-being while managing your responsibilities and demands. By demonstrating the importance of self-care and setting clear boundaries, you serve as an example for your entire school community. Your ability to balance your own well-being promotes overall resilience and creates a supportive environment.

You possess a strong drive for results and achievement. You are focused on accomplishing goals that contribute to the growth and success of your school. By providing clear expectations and setting high standards, you motivate your staff and students to strive for excellence. You understand the significance of tracking progress, celebrating milestones, and adjusting strategies when necessary. Your results-oriented approach ensures that your school remains on a path of continuous improvement.

Your assertiveness, independent thinking, direct communication, effective boundary setting, and results-oriented leadership style set you apart as a decisive and influential leader.

Low Agreeableness: Disadvantages

There are many potential consequences of low agreeableness in leaders, including conflict escalation, difficulty building relationships, less emotional expressiveness, resistance to feedback, and others perceiving their communication as aggressive. In fact, low agreeableness can present certain challenges for you if you aren't aware of them. For example, imagine a scenario where a major change in the school's curriculum is being proposed. You may disregard the concerns and suggestions from teachers, parents, and other stakeholders. Your low agreeableness and inclination towards independence may lead you to make decisions unilaterally, without taking into account the valuable insights and expertise of others, which can lead to strained relationships.

As a low-agreeableness leader, you can inadvertently escalate conflicts within your school communities. To improve this, it is crucial for you to develop strong conflict resolution skills. You should prioritize empathy, active listening, and respect for differing viewpoints. By adopting a more balanced approach, you can navigate disagreements constructively, minimize conflict escalation, and foster healthy relationships among staff, students, and parents.

You may find it challenging to build strong relationships as a low-agreeableness leader, given your assertive and independent nature. However, it is essential to recognize the importance of empathy and active listening in overcoming this difficulty. By being mindful of others' emotions and perspectives, you can establish rapport, build trust, and foster meaningful relationships within your school community. Remember that effective leadership requires assertiveness alongside the ability to cultivate positive and collaborative relationships.

Regarding emotional expressiveness, your tendency to prioritize professionalism and maintain a neutral demeanor may result in less emotional expression. While this contributes to a composed and disciplined environment, it is crucial to acknowledge the value of empathetic and emotionally supportive communication. Especially during challenging times or when individuals require emotional support, the ability to connect on an emotional level can foster trust, enhance motivation, and strengthen relationships.

Another aspect to consider is that you may have a natural inclination to resist feedback or alternative viewpoints. However, maintaining a receptive mindset is crucial for personal and professional growth. It is important to cultivate an openness to receiving feedback, value the input of others, and consider diverse perspectives. Embracing constructive criticism as an opportunity for improvement enhances your leadership effectiveness and creates a culture of continuous development within your school.

The perception of dominance or micromanaging may be associated with your low agreeableness style. This perception can hinder the development of a collaborative and inclusive school environment. To mitigate this, be mindful of your communication style and actively seek input from others. Encourage participation, foster shared decision-making, and value the contributions of all stakeholders. By creating an environment that promotes collaboration, inclusivity, and collective ownership, you can counter the perception of dominance and cultivate a positive school culture.

Understanding the positive and negative attributes associated with high and low agreeableness allows leaders to harness their strengths while mitigating potential challenges. Effective leaders recognize the importance of adapting their leadership style to different situations, cultivating self-awareness, and actively seeking professional development opportunities. By leveraging the power of agreeableness, leaders can create positive, inclusive, and thriving school communities that foster collaboration, empathy, and effective decision-making.

Leveraging Agreeableness for Collaborative School Leadership

It's important to understand the agreeableness trait and how it can impact your relationships with teachers and the overall school environment. When you recognize and appreciate the values that agreeable teachers cherish, like empathy, active listening, and understanding, you can create a positive and productive atmosphere in the school.

◆ **Enhancing Your Teacher–Leader Relationships:** You can adapt your leadership style to establish stronger relationships with your teachers. Appreciating that agreeable teachers value empathy, active listening, and understanding, you can create a supportive and nurturing environment that facilitates effective communication and promotes a positive professional bond. By recognizing their agreeable tendencies, you foster an atmosphere where teachers feel valued and respected, ultimately enhancing your relationships with them.

   Example: *At the beginning of the school year, you gather all teachers and clearly outline your expectations for collaboration on curriculum development. You explain the specific goals you want to achieve, such as aligning the curriculum with new state standards, and how you expect teachers to work together to meet these objectives.*

◆ **Promoting Collaboration and Teamwork:** As someone who values cooperation, empathy, and support for others, you can foster a collaborative and supportive work environment among your teachers. Encourage teamwork, facilitate effective communication, and promote a positive atmosphere where teachers feel comfortable sharing ideas, seeking assistance, and working together towards common goals. By promoting a sense of unity and cooperation, you create a positive and productive work environment for your entire team.

Example: *You create a dedicated online platform or shared workspace where teachers can post their ideas, share resources, and engage in discussions. You actively participate in these discussions, responding to ideas, and encouraging others to join the conversation.*

◆ **Boosting Teacher Morale:** Understanding the agreeableness trait allows you to provide the necessary support and recognition that your agreeable teachers value. By acknowledging their contributions and creating a supportive work environment, you can enhance their motivation and job satisfaction. Recognize their efforts, provide opportunities for growth, and offer a listening ear to their needs. By prioritizing their well-being, you foster a positive and motivating environment for your teachers.

Example: *You regularly acknowledge and celebrate the accomplishments and efforts of your teachers. For instance, you establish a monthly "Teacher Spotlight" program where one teacher is recognized for their exceptional contributions to the school community. Additionally, you offer professional development opportunities tailored to each teacher's interests and career goals. You also create an open-door policy, actively listening to teachers' needs and concerns, and taking action to address them promptly. This approach significantly boosts teacher morale, as they feel valued, supported, and motivated to excel in their roles.*

◆ **Maximizing Teamwork and Synergy:** Most teachers excel in collaborative settings, so capitalize on their strengths. So you can strategically build teams that maximize the strengths of your agreeable teachers. Encourage them to work well with their colleagues, share resources, and actively participate in team projects. By fostering teamwork and synergy, you contribute to improved student outcomes and a more cohesive school community.

Example: *You recognize that some teachers have a knack for teamwork and collaboration. You strategically group them together to lead various school improvement projects, such as* *curriculum development or implementing a new technology initiative. Their synergy not only enhances their job satisfaction but also leads to more innovative approaches and improved student outcomes.*

♦ **Encouraging Open Communication:** Recognize that open communication is vital for effective school leadership. This allows you to encourage your teachers to voice their opinions and concerns freely. Create an inclusive atmosphere where they feel comfortable sharing their thoughts, suggestions, and challenges. By promoting open communication, you foster trust, collaboration, and continual improvement within the school community, positively influencing students, parents, and the wider community.

Example: *You actively encourage teachers to voice their opinions and concerns by holding regular open forums or "town hall" meetings. During these sessions, teachers freely share their thoughts, suggestions, and challenges. You actively listen to their input and take action when necessary, fostering trust, collaboration, and continual improvement within the school community. This approach positively influences students, parents, and the wider community by demonstrating a commitment to transparency and responsiveness.*

Regardless of your agreeableness level, as a leader it is important to be aware and adjust to align with your teacher's needs. You can then promote collaboration, effective conflict resolution, and boost teacher morale. Recognizing their needs and creating a supportive work environment allows you to maximize teamwork and synergy, creating a positive school culture.

Leading Agreeable Educators with Compassion and Balance

In the realm of education, where empathy, kindness, and compassion hold immense value, understanding the significance of these qualities can provide you with a distinct edge as a leader. Many educators are naturally drawn to the teaching profession because of their high levels of agreeableness, making them inherently empathetic and caring individuals. Consequently, as a school leader, demonstrating compassion and understanding towards your teachers becomes paramount. Such actions foster trust, encourage open communication, and cultivate a nurturing environment where teachers feel respected and valued.

Importantly, this compassion takes on added significance when you find yourself in situations where you need to ask your teachers to take on more responsibilities or tasks, especially when you know they may find it challenging to say no or fear speaking up. Acknowledging their agreeable personalities and potential struggles in setting boundaries, your compassionate approach as a leader becomes a valuable asset. It enables you to address their concerns, offer support, and make necessary adjustments with their well-being in mind.

Striking the right balance between assertiveness and compassion empowers you to create a school culture that simultaneously promotes both accountability and emotional well-being. By acknowledging the unique needs and qualities of your teachers, you can play a pivotal role in helping them develop the skills needed for effective boundary-setting and assertiveness. This approach not only enhances job satisfaction among your staff but also fosters positive and collaborative relationships, ultimately cultivating a strong sense of belonging within your educational community. As a leader, this balanced approach sets the stage for continued growth and success, not only for your teachers but for the entire school community, giving you a distinct edge in effective leadership and nurturing a thriving educational environment.

3

Recognizing Risks of Passivity and Aggression in School Leadership

In the world of educational leadership, we often see two distinct approaches – passivity and aggression. These styles may seem quite different, but they share a common problem: they can harm the essential foundations of successful schools. The prevalence of these extremes in educational leadership can be due to various factors, like differing leadership philosophies, personal backgrounds, the unique challenges schools face, and many other reasons that can lead to ineffective leadership.

What's interesting is that leaders often tend to lean towards one of these extremes based on their personality traits. Some leaders naturally lean towards a more passive style, while others may have more aggressive, or domineering, tendencies. These tendencies can influence how leaders make decisions, interact with their teams, and ultimately shape the culture and success of their schools. It's crucial for leaders to reflect on their leadership style to ensure they are the most effective leaders they can be.

Consider the story of a leader we'll call Principal Adams, whose leadership style leaned heavily towards passivity. Within the school, there was a persistent issue with a teacher who consistently arrived late to class. Rather than addressing this problem directly, Principal Adams chose to communicate via a vague email to the entire staff, alluding to punctuality concerns without specifying the teacher involved. This indirect approach, although

DOI: 10.4324/9781032657745-4

well-intentioned, had unintended consequences. It left the rest of the staff bewildered, unsure of the identity of the teacher in question, and unable to offer support or guidance. Morale among the educators dipped as they felt unjustly implicated in an issue they couldn't address effectively. The atmosphere of uncertainty and collective blame became the norm, eroding the once-vibrant spirit of the school. As a result, the school's unity and sense of purpose dwindled, and morale hit an all-time low. The story of Principal Adams serves as a poignant reminder of the perils of passive leadership, where the reluctance to confront specific issues can lead to confusion, frustration, and a loss of direction.

Now, let's envision a different narrative – a school led by Principal Johnson, who embodied an aggressive leadership style. Principal Johnson resorted to calling out the late teacher in public, embarrassing them in front of their colleagues and students. This aggressive approach, although intended to address the punctuality issue directly, had severe and damaging consequences. It created an environment of fear and humiliation, where teachers and staff were afraid to make mistakes or voice concerns, fearing public humiliation.

The teacher who was publicly embarrassed became demoralized and disheartened, leading to a further decline in their performance and morale. Other teachers witnessed this harsh treatment and lived in constant fear of being the next target of Principal Johnson's aggression. The oppressive environment quickly eroded psychological safety, and the creative spirit of both students and educators was smothered. High turnover rates among educators and staff were the glaring indicators of a deep-seated dissatisfaction that permeated every corner of the institution, compromising the very essence of quality education. The story of Principal Johnson illustrates the dark consequences of aggressive leadership, where an overbearing approach can create a toxic environment, driving away talent and stifling innovation.

By examining the stories of Principal Adams and Principal Johnson, we've witnessed the consequences of passive and aggressive leadership. Their tales underscore the importance of finding balance – a leadership style that combines assertiveness and compassion. This balance enables leaders to tackle issues directly while fostering a supportive and respectful environment for all stakeholders. So, let's explore practical strategies and examples to empower you on your journey towards effective and compassionate leadership.

Navigating the Nuances of the Extremes

Before delving into an exploration of these two extremes, it's crucial to recognize that in real-world scenarios, leadership seldom falls exclusively into either the passive or aggressive category. Instead, leaders often demonstrate a blend of behaviors shaped by numerous factors, including their personal philosophies, backgrounds, and the unique challenges facing their educational institutions. These behaviors can manifest as a leader's default approach, profoundly influencing the educational environment's culture and atmosphere.

Gaining insight into these default leadership styles represents a pivotal step towards effective leadership, as they tend to define a leader's primary mode of interaction within the school community. Leaders inclined towards passivity may, without intention, foster an environment that resists necessary change and conflict resolution, potentially impeding growth and innovation. Conversely, leaders leaning predominantly towards aggression may establish an atmosphere characterized by fear and intimidation, stifling creativity and collaboration among team members.

Furthermore, it is imperative to acknowledge that there are circumstances where a degree of passivity or aggression may be appropriate. For instance, a passive leader's proclivity for active listening and avoidance of confrontation can be invaluable when dealing with sensitive personnel matters or seeking input from diverse stakeholders. Similarly, an assertive and decisive leader's traits may prove highly effective in crisis situations or when swift decision-making is of utmost importance.

This nuanced comprehension of leadership styles underscores the significance of adaptability, as educational leadership is inherently dynamic. Leaders must be prepared to adjust their behavior in response to evolving challenges and opportunities.

By recognizing and embracing these complexities, leaders can navigate the intricate terrain of educational leadership more effectively, ultimately contributing to the betterment of their schools, students, and fellow educators.

Understanding Passive Leadership

Passive leadership is a prevalent issue in various organizations, including educational institutions, where leaders often grapple with making challenging decisions, evade conflict, prioritize pleasing others over necessary changes, and encounter difficulties in setting boundaries. This style of leadership frequently originates from a fear of failure or a lack of confidence in one's abilities.

Leaders who exhibit passive leadership traits may project an agreeable and easy-to-work-with image, but their reluctance to take action often results in missed opportunities for growth and improvement. They tend to excessively rely on others for decision-making, creating a void of accountability and contributing to a decline in educational quality.

One of the most noteworthy consequences of passive leadership is the adverse impact on staff morale. When leaders fail to assert themselves and address pressing issues, employees may experience a sense of abandonment and undervaluation. This, in turn, can lead to a decrease in motivation, productivity, and overall job satisfaction among staff members.

Moreover, passive leadership can obstruct effective communication within the organization. Non-confrontational communication styles frequently hinder the timely resolution of significant issues, fostering a culture of avoidance where problems are deferred rather than addressed directly.

Passive leaders may also place an excessive amount of trust in others, a practice that can lead to complacency and a lack of accountability.

Furthermore, passive leadership tends to manifest as a lack of clear direction and vision for the organization. Without a proactive leader to provide guidance, schools may encounter difficulties in establishing goals, implementing necessary changes, and adapting to evolving challenges in the educational landscape. This stagnation can hinder progress and prevent schools from realizing their full potential.

To overcome the pitfalls associated with passive leadership, leaders should endeavor to adopt more proactive and assertive leadership styles. This entails taking ownership of decisions, actively seeking out and addressing conflicts, setting clear boundaries, and fostering open and direct communication.

The Consequences of Passive Leadership on School Culture and Student Outcomes

In education, leadership is the compass guiding institutions toward excellence. However, passive leadership, marked by a lack of accountability and confrontation avoidance, can have significant negative consequences. This section explores the fallout from passive leadership, including lowered standards, reduced motivation, a toxic work atmosphere, and higher staff turnover. These effects create a ripple effect throughout school culture, normalizing mediocrity, hampering student engagement, stifling innovation, and harming long-term student achievement. It's a reminder that proactive leadership is crucial for fostering a culture of excellence and ensuring student success.

- ◆ **Lowered Standards and Expectations:** Passive leadership often fails to set and enforce clear standards and expectations. When leaders do not hold staff and students accountable for their actions and responsibilities, it creates an environment where mediocrity can flourish. Teachers may not be motivated to excel, and students may not strive for academic excellence if they believe that there are no consequences for sub-par performance. As a result, academic achievement can suffer.
- ◆ **Decline in Student Motivation and Achievement:** Without strong leadership, students may lack the motivation to excel academically. When they perceive that their

teachers and school leaders are not committed to their education, it can lead to a sense of apathy and disengagement. This, in turn, negatively affects their academic performance and overall achievement.

◆ **Negative Work Atmosphere:** Passive leadership can contribute to a negative work atmosphere among school staff. When conflicts and tensions are left unresolved due to leaders' avoidance of confrontation, it creates a toxic environment where morale is low and stress is high. Teachers and other staff members may become disheartened and less enthusiastic about their work, impacting their ability to provide quality education.

◆ **Increased Turnover Rates:** A negative work atmosphere resulting from passive leadership can lead to high turnover rates among staff. When employees are dissatisfied with their work environment, they are more likely to seek opportunities elsewhere. High turnover rates can disrupt the stability of a school and hinder the continuity of education for students.

◆ **Avoidance of Critical Issues:** A passive school leader who avoids confronting significant problems within the institution allows issues to fester and escalate. For instance, if a teacher consistently underperforms or engages in misconduct, a passive leader may sidestep the problem, resulting in a decline in educational quality and staff morale.

Passive leadership in schools has a profound and far-reaching impact on school culture and student outcomes. It can lead to lowered standards, decreased motivation, a negative work atmosphere, increased turnover rates, a lack of clear guidance, and feeling that leadership would not duly advocate for staff. These consequences create a ripple effect that normalizes mediocrity, decreases student engagement, stifles innovation, and has long-term implications for student achievement.

To combat these negative effects, educational institutions must prioritize strong, proactive leadership that sets high standards, fosters accountability, and creates a positive and motivating environment for both staff and students. By doing so, schools can cultivate a culture of excellence that propels students toward greater success and personal growth.

Understanding Aggressive Leadership

On the contrary, aggressive school leaders tend to exert control through fear, intimidation, and excessive micromanagement. They often adopt a dictatorial management style, disregarding input from others and making decisions without considering the needs and opinions of the school community. This approach creates a hostile and toxic environment that significantly hinders the teaching and learning process.

Aggressive leaders may use fear as a tool to motivate and control staff, leading to high levels of stress, burnout, and reduced job satisfaction. This, in turn, results in a negative impact on teacher performance and well-being, ultimately affecting the quality of education provided to students. Moreover, a culture of fear and intimidation stifles creativity and innovation, limiting the potential for growth and improvement within the school.

The erosion of psychological safety within a school's structure is a gradual process that occurs when strong leadership transforms into aggressive behavior. It commences with leaders displaying signs of pushiness, gradually escalating into open hostility. This deterioration profoundly affects the foundation of psychological safety, which is vital for creating a positive and productive school environment. This erosion affects students, teachers, and staff on multiple levels, as psychological safety involves feeling trust, respect, and the freedom to express oneself without fear of judgment, mistreatment, or embarrassment. Aggressive leadership disrupts this balance, inducing anxiety and inhibiting the creative spark that should be encouraged. Innovation flourishes when individuals feel safe to take intelligent risks and explore new ideas. However, under aggressive leaders, students and staff become hesitant to venture into uncharted territory. The fear of making mistakes in an environment where leaders are consistently critical becomes a heavy burden that stifles experimentation and innovative solutions. Consequently, brilliant ideas that could thrive in a safe space remain hidden, leaving the school stagnating.

The effects of aggressive leadership extend beyond the school's walls. When diverse perspectives are suppressed, the entire school community misses out on fresh and creative ideas. The absence of varied viewpoints hampers problem-solving from different angles, leading to missed opportunities for growth. Furthermore, there are personal repercussions, as students and staff feel disconnected and out of place. Their inability to contribute freely leads to decreased engagement and commitment, resulting in lower grades, higher turnover, and a pervasive sense of neglect.

In essence, aggressive leadership doesn't merely affect the present; it fosters an environment of fear and tension, stifling risk-taking, open discourse, and individual potential. This impedes the school's capacity to progress and attain its fullest potential. To rectify this situation, leaders must recognize the harm caused by aggressive leadership and work diligently to establish a safe space where creativity and teamwork can flourish, ensuring the school's success in every aspect.

The Consequences of Aggressive Leadership on School Culture and Student Outcomes

Aggressive leadership in educational settings has far-reaching consequences that extend beyond the immediate impact on individuals. It creates a toxic environment that permeates school culture, affecting the well-being of both staff and students. When leaders adopt an aggressive approach, it diminishes morale, fosters fear and anxiety, and erodes trust among the members of the educational community. This, in turn, can lead to negative long-term effects on the institution as a whole. In contrast, leaders who promote a nurturing and collaborative atmosphere tend to foster a positive school culture that encourages student success, personal growth, and overall well-being. Recognizing the detrimental effects of aggressive leadership is crucial, as it allows educational leaders to strive for a more balanced and supportive approach that benefits everyone involved. By prioritizing open communication, collaboration, and a focus on holistic student development, leaders can create a positive and thriving educational environment that not only promotes academic excellence but also nurtures the well-being of staff and students. We will explore some of the significant consequences of aggressive leadership within educational institutions.

- ◆ **Toxic Atmosphere of Fear:** Aggressive leaders often rule with authoritarian tactics, creating an atmosphere of fear and intimidation within the school community. This has several detrimental effects:
  - *Stifled Open Communication:* When fear permeates the environment, individuals are afraid to voice their opinions or concerns. They hesitate to provide feedback or suggest new ideas due to the fear of retaliation or negative consequences.
  - *Hindered Collaboration:* The lack of open communication and trust hampers collaboration among staff members and students. Collaboration is essential for sharing insights, brainstorming innovative solutions, and working together effectively to achieve common goals.
  - *Impaired Creativity:* Fear stifles creativity and innovative thinking. When individuals are constantly on edge, they are less likely to take risks, explore new approaches, or think outside the box. This can lead to a stagnant and unproductive school culture.
- ◆ **High Staff Turnover:** Aggressive leadership often leads to a revolving door of educators and support staff leaving the school. This has far-reaching consequences:
  - *Loss of Experience:* As experienced professionals leave, the school loses valuable expertise and institutional knowledge. This can disrupt the continuity of education and impact the quality of instruction.
  - *Instability:* Constant turnover creates an unstable work environment. Staff members may feel uneasy

and uncertain about the future, leading to decreased morale and productivity. There is a momentum effect that is built from team chemistry that is built over time with the same staff.

- *Difficulty Building Relationships:* Frequent staff turnover makes it challenging to build strong relationships between staff and students. Students may struggle to form lasting connections with their educators, hindering their sense of belonging and support.

◆ **Low Morale among Educators:** Aggressive leadership takes a toll on the morale of educators, resulting in several negative outcomes:

- *Stress and Burnout:* Educators subjected to aggressive leadership often experience high levels of stress and burnout. The constant pressure, fear, and uncertainty about job security can be emotionally and physically exhausting.
- *Decreased Job Satisfaction:* Low morale leads to decreased job satisfaction, which can diminish educators' motivation to go above and beyond in their roles.
- *Impact on Student Outcomes:* When educators are demotivated and emotionally drained, their ability to effectively teach and support students is compromised. This can lead to lower student achievement and hinder overall student outcomes.

◆ **Negative Impact on Teacher–Student Relationships:** A hostile school environment strains the relationships between educators and students in various ways:

- *Limited Trust:* Students may find it difficult to trust educators in such an environment. They may perceive their teachers as authoritarian figures to be feared rather than trusted mentors.
- *Reduced Openness:* The fear and discomfort that students experience around educators can hinder their willingness to seek help or engage in open and meaningful discussions. This limits their access to the

support and guidance they need for academic and personal growth.

◆ **Diminished Student Engagement:** Aggressive leadership has a direct impact on student engagement and enthusiasm for learning:

- *Anxiety and Discomfort:* Students who feel anxious or unsafe due to aggressive leadership are less likely to be engaged in the learning process. They may become disinterested and disengaged from their studies.

- *Lower Academic Performance:* Diminished engagement often leads to lower academic performance as students are less motivated to participate actively in their studies and put forth their best effort.

- *Reduced Motivation:* When students perceive the learning environment as hostile or uninspiring, their motivation to achieve their full potential wanes. This can have long-term consequences on their educational and personal development.

The toxic atmosphere of fear that aggressive leadership creates stifles communication, leads to high staff turnover, and diminishes morale among educators. Moreover, it strains teacher–student relationships and hampers student engagement and innovation in the classroom. Recognizing these consequences is imperative for educational leaders, as they shape not only the immediate experiences of staff and students but also the long-term success and well-being of the institution.

Balancing Leadership Styles in Educational Institutions

The ability to balance contrasting leadership styles stands as a hallmark of effective leadership. Education leaders are not confined to rigid categories of passive or aggressive; rather, they embody a spectrum of traits influenced by personal philosophies, experiences, and the distinctive challenges faced by their institutions. This balance involves seamlessly integrating diverse leadership behaviors, informed by research, self-reflection, and collaboration, to promote a thriving educational environment.

Leadership Spectrum: Navigating a Multidimensional Landscape

Recognizing the multidimensional nature of leadership is paramount for educational leaders. Rather than constraining themselves to a fixed, singular leadership style, effective leaders perceive themselves as capable of navigating a broad spectrum of behaviors. This understanding empowers them to tailor their leadership approach to the specific context they face, whether it demands a gentle touch or a firmer stance.

Example: Imagine a principal overseeing a school facing declining enrollment and struggling student performance. Recognizing the need for change, the principal shifts from a predominantly passive approach, which had been focused on collaboration and consensus-building, to a more assertive one. They take decisive action by implementing evidence-based instructional strategies, offering targeted support to teachers, and engaging with parents to address their concerns. This strategic shift enables the school to adapt to its challenges effectively.

Strategic Flexibility: The Art of Timely Adaptation

Effective educational leaders exhibit strategic flexibility. They possess the ability to discern when to employ different leadership styles judiciously. They understand that a passive approach, with its emphasis on listening and collaboration, can foster innovation and inclusivity. Conversely, moments requiring decisiveness and assertiveness may call for a more active, assertive stance.

Example: Consider a department chair in a university facing a contentious faculty meeting regarding curriculum changes. Understanding the need for collaboration and consensus, the chair initially adopts a passive leadership approach, encouraging open dialogue and seeking input from all faculty members. However, when discussions become unproductive and divergent, the chair pivots to a more assertive stance. They make a well-reasoned decision based on input received, effectively bringing the meeting to a productive conclusion.

Cultivating a Leadership Blend: Crafting a Harmonious Symphony

Creating a balanced blend of leadership styles can be likened to crafting a fine piece of music. Each note represents a different aspect of leadership, and the art lies in striking the right chord at the right time to produce a symphony of success. Leaders should aim to seamlessly transition between passive and aggressive elements, ensuring their leadership composition resonates with their team, students, and the institution as a whole.

Example: In the context of a school principal's leadership, imagine a situation where a new inclusive education program is being introduced. Initially, the principal takes a passive approach by inviting input from teachers, parents, and specialists to shape the program. Once the program's framework is established, the principal switches to an assertive mode by implementing clear guidelines and expectations for its successful execution. This balanced blend of leadership styles fosters collaboration during the program's development and ensures effective execution afterward.

Empathy and Adaptability: The Connective Tissue of Leadership

Empathy serves as the connective tissue in leadership balance. Understanding the diverse perspectives and emotions of team members, students, and stakeholders lays the foundation for effective leadership. Coupled with adaptability, empathy allows leaders to pivot gracefully between styles and tailor their leadership to the needs of the moment.

Example: Picture a school leader dealing with a student who is struggling academically due to personal issues. Initially, the leader adopts a passive, empathetic approach, listening attentively to the student's concerns and providing emotional support. However, when it becomes clear that immediate intervention is required to address the academic challenges, the leader shifts to an assertive mode by collaborating with teachers and parents to implement a tailored support plan. This empathetic adaptability ensures the student receives the necessary help while maintaining their emotional well-being.

Building a Culture of Collaboration: Fostering Collective Success

Leadership balance extends beyond the leader themselves; it permeates the entire institution. Leaders should actively foster a culture of collaboration where individuals are encouraged to contribute their unique strengths and perspectives. In such an environment, the balanced blend of leadership styles flourishes organically, contributing to the institution's overall success.

Example: Think of a university dean working to enhance interdisciplinary research among faculty members. The dean takes a proactive approach by creating a collaborative platform where researchers from diverse departments can share their expertise. This culture of collaboration encourages faculty members to combine their knowledge and approaches, resulting in groundbreaking research projects that benefit the institution and society at large.

Continuous Learning: The Ongoing Journey

Similar to how musicians hone their craft through practice and exploration, educational leaders must commit to continuous learning. Staying attuned to emerging educational trends, seeking feedback grounded in empirical evidence, and refining their leadership composition ensures they remain effective and responsive to the ever-changing educational landscape.

Example: An educational superintendent actively engages in professional development, attending leadership workshops and conferences regularly. In doing so, they stay current with the latest educational research and leadership best practices. Additionally, they solicit feedback from teachers, parents, and students to adapt their leadership style continuously, ensuring that it aligns with the evolving needs of their school district. This commitment to ongoing learning and adaptation keeps the educational institution on a trajectory of improvement and success.

4

The Power of Assertiveness in School Leadership

A compelling movie scene that beautifully exemplifies the embodiment of assertiveness in a school leader is found in the film *Dead Poets Society* (1989). In this particular scene, Mr. Nolan confronts the English teacher Mr. Keating, portrayed by actor Robin Williams, regarding his unorthodox teaching methods.

Throughout the scene, Mr. Nolan demonstrates assertiveness by addressing his concerns in a direct and respectful manner. He effectively communicates the school's expectations and stresses the importance of adhering to the established curriculum. Mr. Nolan's demeanor remains calm and composed, showcasing his confidence in his role as a leader.

Crucially, Mr. Nolan actively listens to Mr. Keating's perspective, genuinely considering his viewpoint before reaching a final decision. Mr. Nolan engages in a constructive dialogue, allowing space for Mr. Keating to express his ideas while maintaining the boundaries and guidelines set by the school.

This scene highlights several key characteristics of assertiveness:

♦ **Clear communication:** Mr. Nolan articulates the school's expectations and concerns with clarity, ensuring that his message is understood by Mr. Keating.

DOI: 10.4324/9781032657745-5

- ◆ **Respect for oneself and others:** Mr. Nolan demonstrates respect for his own role as the leader and the importance of the established curriculum, while also acknowledging and considering Mr. Keating's perspective.
- ◆ **Confidence:** Mr. Nolan's confident demeanor reflects his belief in his position as school leader, allowing him to express himself without belittling or undermining Mr. Keating.
- ◆ **Active listening:** Mr. Nolan actively listens to Mr. Keating's perspective, displaying empathy and a genuine interest in understanding his point of view.
- ◆ **Non-aggressive expression:** Mr. Nolan conveys his concerns assertively, refraining from resorting to aggression, hostility, or disrespect.
- ◆ **Boundary setting:** Mr. Nolan establishes and upholds the boundaries of the school's curriculum and expectations, while also fostering a space for constructive dialogue.

This scene underscores the significance of assertiveness in educational leadership, showcasing how someone can effectively balance the need for adherence to school guidelines without being authoritarian or controlling. It serves as a powerful example of how assertiveness can be utilized to address conflicts and concerns in a respectful and productive manner, ultimately leading to improved communication and understanding within the school community.

What Does It Mean to Embody Assertiveness as a School Leader?

One common misconception about assertiveness that I have observed in 30 years in the educational field is that it's often mistaken for aggression, rudeness, or lack of empathy. However, assertiveness is distinct from these behaviors. In fact, I know many educators who don't even like to use or hear the word because it conjures up negative thoughts and feelings. However, assertiveness does not involve being aggressive, dominating others, showing disrespect, or disregarding their feelings and rights. It's worth noting that in the above scene, Mr. Nolan refrains from resorting to aggression, hostility, or disrespect. Instead, he conveys his concerns assertively, focusing on the issues at hand rather than attacking the person.

Assertiveness involves the ability to express thoughts, feelings, opinions, needs, and boundaries directly and respect-fully. It represents a middle ground between passivity, where one's voice may go unheard, and aggression, where others' feelings are disregarded. In this nuanced approach, assertive leaders not only consider the perspectives and emotions of others but also value themselves as individuals with valid viewpoints and needs. This balanced approach fosters constructive dia-logue, mutual understanding, and the pursuit of common goals within the school community. Being assertive involves several key characteristics and behaviors:

◆ **Clear Communication:** Assertive leaders prioritize clear communication by using direct and concise lan-guage. Their messages leave no room for vagueness or misunderstanding, ensuring that they are easily under-stood by others.

◆ **Respect for Oneself and Others:** Assertiveness involves striking a delicate balance between recognizing and respecting one's own needs and rights while also acknow-ledging those of others. It entails advocating for oneself while valuing the perspectives and boundaries of fellow individuals.

◆ **Confidence:** Assertive leaders exude confidence in both their abilities and opinions. They possess a strong belief in their self-worth and express themselves confidently, all the while ensuring that this confidence does not diminish the worth of others.

◆ **Active Listening:** Assertiveness is closely linked to active listening. Assertive leaders pay keen attention to others, demonstrating empathy and a genuine interest in understanding diverse viewpoints.

◆ **Non-Aggressive Expression:** It's vital to distinguish assertiveness from aggression. Assertive leaders express themselves firmly but without resorting to hostility, intimidation, or disrespect. They convey their thoughts and feelings assertively while avoiding any form of aggressive or confrontational behavior.

◆ **Boundary Setting:** Assertiveness encompasses the skill of establishing and maintaining personal boundaries. This entails effectively communicating limits, confidently saying "no" when necessary, and respecting the boundaries set by others.

◆ **Conflict Resolution:** Assertive leaders excel in resolving conflicts constructively. They approach conflicts with a problem-solving mindset, seeking mutually beneficial solutions that consider the needs and feelings of all parties involved.

Developing assertiveness as a leader offers a range of benefits. It improves classroom management, enhances communication with students, balances authority with empathy, and promotes collaboration with colleagues and parents. Assertiveness also aids in stress management and supports professional growth.

By embracing assertiveness, leaders can establish clear classroom expectations, communicate effectively with students, and foster positive learning environments. This approach facilitates productive collaborations, maintains work–life balance, and empowers leaders to advocate for themselves, seek professional development, and excel in their roles. Ultimately, assertiveness empowers leaders to create thriving educational communities and nurture their own growth.

Strategies to Develop Assertiveness Skills

Self-reflection is a critical step in developing assertiveness skills. It involves introspection and gaining a deep understanding of one's communication style, strengths, and weaknesses. By taking the time to reflect on personal interactions, educators can identify areas that require improvement and implement strategies to enhance assertiveness. Self-reflection provides a foundation for growth and development, fostering effective communication with students and colleagues alike. Engaging in self-reflection is a fundamental step towards developing assertiveness skills. Take the time to gain insights into your communication style and identify areas where assertiveness can be improved. Recognize specific situations or interactions that require enhancement and take targeted action accordingly. By understanding your strengths and weaknesses, you can develop strategies to assertively communicate in different scenarios.

To promote a structured and respectful classroom environment, it is essential to effectively communicate expectations, rules, and boundaries to all stakeholders from the beginning. Ensure their understanding of what is expected of them and the consequences of not meeting those expectations. By setting clear expectations, you establish a foundation for assertive communication and facilitate a positive learning environment.

Practicing assertive communication techniques is key to expressing yourself confidently while respecting others. Use "I" statements to express needs and concerns calmly and directly. Active listening is also crucial in assertive communication, allowing you to understand your staff's perspectives. By using these techniques, you can address challenges effectively and foster open and respectful dialogue.

Learning to manage emotions effectively is essential for assertive communication. When faced with challenging situations, take a moment to pause, breathe, and think before responding. This prevents reactive responses and allows you to respond assertively and constructively. Emotional management promotes a calm and confident demeanor, enabling you to handle conflicts and challenges assertively.

Building self-confidence is crucial for assertive communication. Educators can engage in personal development activities such as self-reflection and positive self-talk. By recognizing their strengths as educators and celebrating their achievements, they can cultivate a sense of self-assurance. Increased self-confidence empowers educators to be more assertive in their communication and actions, creating a positive impact on their interactions with students and colleagues.

Developing active listening skills is essential for assertive communication. By actively listening to students' perspectives and concerns, you demonstrate empathy and understanding. This enables you to respond assertively, address their needs effectively, and foster a supportive learning environment. Active listening enhances communication and builds trust between educators and students.

Regularly seeking feedback from colleagues or mentors is invaluable in refining assertiveness skills. Feedback provides insights into how you come across in different situations and helps identify areas for improvement. By actively seeking feedback, you can continuously enhance your assertiveness and adapt your communication style to better meet the needs of your students.

The Benefits of Assertiveness in School Leadership

Assertiveness assumes a role of utmost significance. It stands as a cornerstone of strength, supporting school leaders in their quest for effective decision-making, open communication, and crisis management. The following six critical benefits of assertiveness form the bedrock of leadership, creating an atmosphere where conflicts find resolution, accountability is upheld, and teacher development thrives. Through practical examples, we delve into the heart of assertiveness, showcasing its indispensable role in shaping the educational landscape. Join us as we navigate the assertive path to leadership success in the world of schools, where the impact of assertiveness cannot be overstated.

♦ **Effective Decision-Making:** Assertive leaders excel in decision-making. They gather relevant information, consider input from stakeholders, and make choices that align with the school's mission and goals. This benefit ensures that the school progresses in a purposeful direction.

Example: *A principal faced with a decision regarding the allocation of resources carefully analyzes academic data, consults with teachers, and decides to invest in additional resources for a struggling student support program. This decision aligns with the school's goal of improving student outcomes.*

◆ **Open Communication:** Assertive leaders foster open and transparent communication within the school community. They encourage honest discussions, actively listen to diverse viewpoints, and create an atmosphere where ideas and concerns can be freely expressed.

Example: *A superintendent holds regular town hall meetings with parents, teachers, and community members to discuss important school matters. During these meetings they actively listen to concerns, answer questions, and seek input, fostering a culture of open communication.*

◆ **Conflict Resolution:** Assertiveness equips leaders with the skills to address conflicts and challenges constructively. They mediate disputes, facilitate dialogue, and find resolutions that maintain positive relationships and harmony within the school.

Example: *A school principal mediates a disagreement between two teachers regarding classroom resources. They facilitate a productive conversation, helping the teachers identify a fair allocation plan that satisfies both parties and preserves a collaborative work environment.*

◆ **Accountability:** Assertive leaders hold themselves and their team members accountable for meeting expectations and delivering results. This accountability ensures that everyone is committed to achieving the school's goals.

Example: *A department head sets clear performance expectations for their team of teachers and regularly reviews progress. When a teacher falls behind on curriculum delivery, the department head provides support and resources to help the teacher catch up, emphasizing accountability for all.*

◆ **Teacher Development:** Assertive leaders actively support the professional growth and development of teachers. They identify areas for improvement, provide constructive feedback, and offer guidance and resources to help educators excel.

Example: *A school principal conducts regular classroom observations and provides detailed feedback to teachers. When identifying a need for improvement in a specific teaching technique, the principal arranges for the teacher to attend a professional development workshop focused on that skill.*

◆ **Managing Crises:** In times of crisis or challenging situations, assertive leaders can make critical decisions quickly and effectively. They remain composed, prioritize safety and well-being, and take actions to manage crises efficiently.

Example: *During a sudden health crisis, a school principal swiftly implements safety protocols, communicates transparently with parents and staff, and coordinates with health authorities. Their assertive crisis management ensures the health and safety of the school community.*

Utilizing Your Assertiveness Edge

Assertiveness is an invaluable tool that empowers school leaders to navigate the complex web of responsibilities, expectations, and challenges that come their way. We've already explored the myriad benefits of assertiveness in leadership, recognizing how it contributes to effective communication, confident decision-making, and the establishment of a culture built on trust and collaboration. Now, let's delve into the practical realm of assertiveness, examining real-life scenarios that school leaders frequently encounter. From faculty meetings to parent-teacher conferences, budget allocation to disciplinary matters, and negotiations with stakeholders to implementing change, assertiveness plays a pivotal role in guiding these interactions towards productive outcomes.

In each of these day-to-day situations, assertiveness is about striking a delicate balance. It involves respecting the diverse perspectives of those you lead while confidently expressing your own needs, expectations, and decisions. The aim is not dominance, but rather the creation of an environment where open dialogue and constructive collaboration flourish. As we explore these practical examples of assertiveness, you will gain insights into how to handle these situations with grace, confidence, and effectiveness, ultimately fostering a culture of open communication within your educational institution. As we leave this chapter, let's review some practical examples of what assertiveness looks like day-to-day for a school leader:

◆ **Faculty Meetings:**
  • Situation: Leading discussions with differing opinions and ideas.
  • Action: Encourage open discussion and express your expectations for a respectful and constructive dialogue. Use "I" statements to express your viewpoint and facilitate collaborative decision-making.
◆ **Student Discipline Issues:**
  • Situation: Addressing student discipline issues with parents and teachers.
  • Action: Present a balanced perspective, emphasizing the importance of fairness and consistency. Clearly communicate the consequences of disciplinary actions while being open to parents' concerns.
◆ **Staff Performance Reviews:**
  • Situation: Providing feedback to teachers and staff members.
  • Action: Offer constructive feedback in a respectful but direct manner. Use specific examples and focus on behaviors or actions rather than personal attributes.
◆ **Seeking Support from Superiors:**
  • Situation: Advocating for additional resources or support from higher-ups.
  • Action: Present a well-prepared case, emphasizing the positive impact of the requested support on the school's goals and outcomes. Be confident and persistent in pursuing what is necessary for your school's success.

♦ **Handling Difficult Conversations:**
  - Situation: Dealing with confrontational or emotionally charged conversations.
  - Action: Stay calm and composed during challenging conversations. Focus on active listening and empathy, but also take assertive actions to express your own needs and boundaries as necessary to maintain a productive dialogue.

In all these situations, assertiveness involves a balanced approach that respects others' perspectives while confidently expressing your own needs, expectations, and decisions. Developing assertiveness skills and applying them in these contexts will help school leaders effectively navigate challenges, build trust, and foster a culture of open communication within their educational institutions.

5

The EQ Edge

Maximizing Your Emotional Intelligence

A school leader's capacity to connect with people on an emotional level has emerged as the most potent predictor of leadership potential and effectiveness. In essence, emotional intelligence (EQ) stands as a defining trait of exceptional leaders. As a school leader aspiring to succeed, your EQ might be the most influential aspect of your leadership. The good news is that even if you don't possess the highest natural EQ, it's a skill that can be cultivated with dedicated effort.

Think back to the leaders who left a lasting impact on you. Were they exceptional budget managers, or did you think, "This school leader truly knows how to create an effective learning environment!" Chances are, it wasn't their managerial prowess that inspired you; it was the intangible qualities like motivation, inspiration, and feeling appreciated. High EQ school leaders take the time to ask teachers personal questions like, "How are you? How's your family? How can I support you?" They strive to establish personal connections with their staff. Some individuals might struggle with the emotional side of leadership, and these are often the ones who find it challenging to secure their staff's commitment. It's crucial to recognize that when dealing with people, we're not

DOI: 10.4324/9781032657745-6

dealing with creatures of pure logic; we're dealing with beings driven by emotions. In fact, most of our decisions are emotionally motivated, with logic often serving as a post hoc justification. Therefore, how you express and connect with the emotions of your staff can be the linchpin that separates success from failure. Remember that forging emotional connections captures the hearts of your staff and fosters a committed team.

In the realm of emotional intelligence, the first step is mastering your own emotions. School leaders cannot maintain respect when their reactions to situations are unpredictable. School leaders who exhibit erratic emotional states tend not to thrive in their roles. Hence, learning to manage your emotions is the foundational step in building robust, positive relationships with your staff. Indeed, before you can lead others, you must first lead yourself. While there are several facets to developing high EQ, these four key elements will significantly accelerate your ability to connect with others effectively.

Mastering Emotional Intelligence

Effective leadership goes beyond administrative tasks and curriculum management. It requires a deep understanding of emotions, relationships, and self-awareness. This section explores the four critical domains of emotional intelligence: self-awareness, self-management, social awareness, and relationship management, and their pivotal roles in successful school leadership.

Whether you're an aspiring school leader preparing for your role or an experienced educator looking to enhance your leadership abilities, this section will empower you in leading authentically, cultivating a positive school culture, and driving meaningful change within your educational community.

1. Self-Awareness

Self-awareness involves recognizing your emotions and their impact on others, a key component of emotional intelligence (EQ). It enables you to manage your emotions by evaluating them. This trait comprises emotional awareness and self-confidence. Some leaders may struggle with understanding how they are perceived by others, but self-awareness is crucial for personal growth and enhanced performance, as it helps identify areas for improvement and effective delegation of tasks.

Practical Steps for School Leaders to Cultivate Greater Self-Awareness

- ◆ **Engage in Reflective Practices:** Dedicate time in your busy schedule to self-reflection. Whether through journaling, meditation, or contemplative walks, engage in practices that prompt you to scrutinize your thoughts, feelings, and reactions.
- ◆ **Seek Constructive Feedback:** Actively solicit feedback from colleagues, mentors, and trusted individuals within your school community. Constructive feedback can offer invaluable insights into your leadership style and areas for personal growth.
- ◆ **Embrace Vulnerability:** Be open to acknowledging your vulnerabilities and limitations. Understand that you are not infallible, and recognize that self-awareness begins with a candid assessment of your strengths and weaknesses.
- ◆ **Engage in Emotional Journaling:** Maintain a dedicated journal for documenting your emotional experiences. Recording your feelings and the circumstances that trigger them can help you discern patterns and gain clarity regarding your emotional responses.
- ◆ **Utilize 360-Degree Assessments:** Leverage 360-degree assessments that collect feedback from peers, subordinates, and superiors. This comprehensive perspective provides a well-rounded view of your leadership style and its impact.
- ◆ **Regular Self-Assessment:** Periodically evaluate your goals, values, and aspirations. Reflect on whether your current leadership approach aligns with these ideals, and adapt your strategies accordingly.

By actively pursuing self-awareness, school leaders lay a robust foundation for authentic, empathetic, and effective leadership. The journey of self-discovery extends beyond the personal sphere; it represents a profound commitment to the overall improvement and flourishing of the school community as a whole.

2. Self-Regulation

Self-regulation entails the skill to handle disruptive emotions and impulses like fear, anxiety, anger, and sadness. It involves thinking before acting and taking responsibility for your actions. While you may not control when emotions arise, you can influence their duration through certain steps for school leaders seeking to become better self-managers.

Practical Steps for School Leaders to Cultivate Greater Self-Regulation

♦ **Emotional Awareness:** Regularly check in with yourself to identify your emotional state. Pay attention to the emotions that arise in different situations and understand their triggers. Journaling can be a helpful tool for tracking your emotional responses.

♦ **Mindfulness and Meditation:** Incorporate mindfulness practices and meditation into your daily routine. These techniques can help you stay present, reduce stress, and gain better control over your emotional reactions.

♦ **Pause and Reflect:** Before reacting to a situation, take a moment to pause and reflect. Consider the potential consequences of your actions and whether they align with your goals and values. This pause allows you to respond more thoughtfully rather than reacting impulsively.

♦ **Stress Management:** Develop effective stress management strategies. This could involve regular exercise, proper nutrition, sufficient sleep, and relaxation techniques. When you're less stressed, it's easier to regulate your emotions.

♦ **Self-Care:** Prioritize self-care as an essential component of self-management. Regularly engage in activities that rejuvenate your mind and body, fostering resilience and emotional well-being.

◆ **Continuous Learning:** Commit to ongoing self-improvement. Seek out resources, workshops, and training opportunities that empower you with the knowledge and tools necessary to enhance your self-management skills.

◆ **Self-Management** is pivotal for school leaders, as it involves controlling emotions, fostering a supportive environment, and necessitates introspective reflection. It's a journey of self-mastery that directly impacts the success and harmony of the entire educational community.

3. Social Awareness

Social awareness in school leadership involves understanding and empathizing with the emotions and needs of all stakeholders in the school community. It encompasses recognizing social dynamics, cultural diversity, and the feelings of students, teachers, staff, parents, and community members. Socially aware leaders use this understanding to inform their decisions, promote equity, diversity, inclusion, and create a culture of belonging.

Key traits for social awareness include empathy, active listening, and cultural competence. Empathy fosters trust and open communication, active listening helps address issues effectively, and cultural competence promotes inclusivity and values diversity.

Steps for School Leaders to Enhance Social Awareness

◆ **Active Listening:** Practice active listening skills when engaging with students, teachers, parents, and other stakeholders. Make a conscious effort to fully under-stand their perspectives and feelings without judgment or interruption.

◆ **Empathy Development:** Cultivate empathy by putting yourself in others' shoes. Consider their experiences, challenges, and emotions to gain a deeper understanding of their needs and concerns.

◆ **Cultural Competency:** Invest in cultural competency training to better understand and appreciate the diverse backgrounds and perspectives within your school community. Foster an inclusive environment that values and celebrates diversity.

- **Stakeholder Engagement:** Actively engage with various stakeholders through regular meetings, open forums, and surveys. Encourage feedback and input to gain insights into their expectations and concerns.
- **Community Involvement:** Participate in community events, meetings, and partnerships. Connect with local organizations and parents to better grasp the broader context and needs of your school's community.
- **Observe Non-Verbal Cues:** During interactions, pay attention to non-verbal cues, such as body language and facial expressions. These cues can provide valuable insights into the emotions and thoughts of others.
- **Conflict Resolution Skills:** Develop strong conflict resolution skills. Address conflicts promptly and constructively, seeking mutually beneficial solutions that consider the well-being of all parties involved.
- **Mentorship and Feedback:** Seek mentorship or coaching from experienced leaders who can provide guidance and feedback on your social awareness skills. Continuously strive for improvement and self-awareness.

By embracing social awareness, school leaders can foster a culture of empathy, understanding, and inclusivity within their educational communities. These skills not only enhance relationships but also promote effective leadership, collaborative problem-solving, and the overall well-being of the school ecosystem. It is a journey that propels school leaders toward greater connection and effectiveness in their roles.

4. Relationship Management

Relationship management involves understanding and responding to the emotional complexities of individuals. It's a crucial skill for success in both personal and professional life, especially in today's highly connected world. It includes abilities such as persuasion, driving change, and fostering collective synergy. Effective leaders with high emotional intelligence (EQ) can influence, communicate effectively, manage conflicts, and build rapport.

True leadership doesn't equate to excessive emotional displays but rather involves regulating emotions to engage and inspire others. Effective leaders establish emotional connections, drawing people in through positivity and optimism. This fosters a culture where team members are motivated to deliver their best efforts. Key elements of this skill set include empathetic communication, conflict resolution, and mediation skills, as well as active listening and providing constructive feedback.

Steps for School Leaders to Enhance Relationship Management

- ◆ **Open and Transparent Communication:** Foster open, honest, and transparent communication with all stakeholders, including students, parents, teachers, and staff. Ensure that everyone feels heard and valued.
- ◆ **Active Engagement:** Actively engage with individuals in your school community. Attend school events, meetings, and extracurricular activities to demonstrate your commitment and support.
- ◆ **Relationship Building:** Make a conscious effort to build and maintain relationships. Show genuine interest in the lives and well-being of others. Remember important details about individuals to strengthen connections.
- ◆ **Conflict Resolution Skills:** Develop strong conflict resolution skills. Approach conflicts with a problem-solving mindset and a focus on maintaining positive relationships.
- ◆ **Collaborative Leadership:** Promote collaborative leadership by involving stakeholders in decision-making processes. Seek input, encourage participation, and create a sense of shared ownership.
- ◆ **Empower Others:** Empower and support your team members, teachers, and staff in their professional growth. Provide opportunities for skill development and recognize their contributions.
- ◆ **Feedback Loops:** Establish feedback mechanisms to gather input and insights from the school community. Act on feedback to improve processes and relationships.

♦ **Mentoring and Coaching:** Consider mentoring or coaching programs within your school to facilitate professional development and relationship-building among staff and students.

♦ **Conflict Prevention:** Implement strategies to proactively prevent conflicts by promoting a culture of respect, empathy, and collaboration within the school community.

♦ **Lead by Example:** Demonstrate the values and behaviors you wish to see in others. Your leadership sets the tone for the entire school community.

By actively managing relationships, school leaders can create an environment where trust and collaboration thrive, enabling the entire educational community to flourish. These skills not only enhance teamwork and cooperation but also contribute to a positive school culture and the long-term success of the institution. It is a journey that empowers leaders to be catalysts for positive change and transformation within their schools.

Elevating Your Emotional Intelligence Edge

Emotional intelligence (EQ) is not a fixed trait; it's a dynamic skill that can be developed and strengthened with consistent practice. Your brain possesses the remarkable ability to form and refine neural connections between rational and emotional centers as you work on your EQ. This process enhances the flow of information within your brain, allowing you to become more emotionally intelligent over time (Bradberry, 2009).

Research consistently demonstrates a direct link between emotionally intelligent leadership and positive outcomes like employee satisfaction, retention, and performance. Therefore, it's paramount to prioritize EQ as a core element of your leadership development, especially when striving to build deeper connections with your faculty. Here are strategies, inspired by insights from *Psychology Today* (Rosenthal, 2012), to boost your EQ and, consequently, elevate your overall effectiveness:

◆ **Reflect on Your Emotions:** Initiate the journey by examining your emotional responses in various situations. Consider how you react when a teacher faces frustration or when your decisions are questioned. Identifying your emotions and reactions enhances self-awareness, a fundamental step toward emotional control. *Example:* When a teacher expresses frustration about a curriculum change, pause and ask yourself why you're feeling defensive. This reflection can help you respond more empathetically and constructively.

◆ **Seek Comprehensive Feedback:** Acknowledge that others may perceive you differently than you perceive yourself. The goal isn't to establish right or wrong but to gain invaluable insights into how you and others view each other. Encourage your teachers to provide anonymous online feedback or engage in one-on-one discussions to gather input on specific situations. Specific feedback is instrumental for growth. *Example:* After implementing a new policy with mixed reactions, gather anonymous online feedback or hold one-on-one discussions with teachers to understand their perspectives and make informed adjustments.

◆ **Listen to Your Body:** Tune in to physical sensations like a knot in your stomach during your daily commute; they often signal sources of stress. Acknowledging these sensations and the underlying feelings they represent allows you to engage your rational mind in processing them, preventing impulsive emotional reactions. *Example:* During a stressful time like the start of the school year, notice physical tension during your daily commute. Acknowledge it and consider what might be causing the stress, helping you address stressors proactively.

◆ **Know When to Shift Focus:** Recognize when introspection has fulfilled its purpose, and it's time to direct your attention outward. Prolonged dwelling on negative emotions can amplify them. Emotional intelligence encompasses both introspection and engagement with the world around you. This is especially vital when addressing complex issues with teachers or managing school-related challenges. Once the problem is addressed, pivot your focus away from negativity to maintain your emotional well-being. *Example:* After a challenging discussion with a teacher, shift your focus away from dwelling on negative emotions. Redirect your attention to other tasks or interactions to maintain your emotional well-being.

◆ **Embrace the Power of the Pause:** Incorporate the practice of the "pregnant pause," a moment to reflect before speaking or acting. Widespread adoption of this practice can lead to more concise emails, efficient meetings, and reduced inflammatory comments on social media. In conversations, the pause offers a valuable opportunity to contemplate an issue or topic before reacting emotionally, fostering improved communication and decision-making. *Example:* In a discussion with a parent concerned about a school policy, take a brief pause after they express their grievances. Use this moment to reflect on their perspective before responding. This pause can lead to a more empathetic and effective conversation, ultimately strengthening the parent–school relationship.

The mastery of emotional intelligence, often referred to as EQ, is not just a journey; it's a game-changer for school leaders. EQ encompasses self-awareness, self-regulation, empathy, social skills, and motivation, all of which are pivotal in leadership effectiveness. By embracing self-reflection, seeking feedback, practicing mindfulness, and fostering emotional balance, school leaders can ascend to a level of effectiveness that transcends the ordinary.

One of the key advantages of developing high emotional intelligence as a school leader is the ability to forge bonds of trust within the educational community. When leaders are attuned to their own emotions and those of others, they can connect on a deeper level with teachers, students, and parents. This trust forms the foundation of open and honest communication, which is essential for a thriving learning environment.

Furthermore, leaders with high EQ excel at inspiring collaboration among their teams. They understand the diverse emotional needs and strengths of their staff, enabling them to create an environment where every member of the school community can thrive. These leaders can resolve conflicts effectively, promote teamwork, and encourage creativity and innovation.

Importantly, emotional intelligence is not a fixed attribute; it's a dynamic and invaluable asset that school leaders can continuously refine and leverage to their advantage. By incorporating EQ into their leadership approach, school leaders can ensure lasting positive impacts on their schools and the lives of those they serve. Ultimately, EQ gives school leaders a powerful edge in becoming highly effective leaders who foster a culture of growth, collaboration, and well-being within their educational institutions.

6

The Power of Compassion in Leadership

Compassion in educational leadership is of paramount importance, particularly considering the way teachers are perceived and treated in society. Despite their crucial and challenging roles, educators often find themselves underappreciated and undervalued. Recognizing this, compassionate leadership becomes a vital element in creating a supportive and nurturing educational environment.

Teachers are often viewed as caregivers, mentors, and role models, embodying qualities of warmth, kindness, and a sincere commitment to their students' well-being. These educators routinely provide affirmation, support, and encouragement to their students. However, it's equally important to acknowledge that teachers, like their students, require affirmation and compassion in return.

Consider the story of my good friend Mr. Z. He wasn't just a friend, but he was also an inspiring, compassionate principal. He passed away a few years ago from cancer, but his memory lives on through the stories we share about his remarkable character.

One such story that deeply resonates with me is a testament to his compassionate leadership. Several of the teachers at his school had children attending the nearby elementary school. Instead of expecting these dedicated educators to drop their children off

DOI: 10.4324/9781032657745-7

early at their school and wait for the elementary school to open, Mr. Z came up with a simple yet heartfelt solution.

He allowed the teachers to bring their children into their own classrooms at the middle school. There, these young ones could stay comfortably, play, and engage in quiet activities until it was time for them to go to their respective elementary school. Mr. Z understood that balancing work and family life was challenging for his staff, and this small gesture of kindness was his way of making their lives a bit easier.

But Mr. Z's compassion didn't stop there. When it was time for the elementary school day to begin, he took it upon himself to drive these children over on a school bus. His mornings were dedicated to ensuring that his teachers' children reached their school safely and on time.

Mr. Z's actions went beyond just logistical convenience; they showcased his deep understanding of the needs of his staff. His willingness to accommodate them not only made him beloved but also instilled a sense of loyalty and dedication among his teachers. They knew that Mr. Z had their backs, and there wasn't anything they wouldn't do for him because of his kindness.

As time passed, Mr. Z's legacy of compassion continued to inspire those who had the privilege of knowing him. The bond he forged between his teachers, their children, and the school community remained strong, a testament to the enduring power of simple acts of kindness. It was a reflection of the man behind the title, a dear friend whose memory would forever be cherished for the warmth, understanding, and compassion he brought into our lives.

This kind of compassionate leadership encourages a sense of community and collaboration among both staff and students. By cultivating an environment where everyone feels supported, respected, and valued, leaders can shape a positive school culture that promotes teamwork, cooperation, and collective growth. This collaborative approach not only elevates student learning but also nurtures a sense of belonging and connectedness within the educational community.

Compassion is an indispensable quality for school leaders to embody, especially in recognizing the vital role teachers play and the challenges they face. By practicing compassion, leaders can establish a nurturing and supportive environment that fosters positive relationships, student engagement, and overall well-being. When leaders prioritize compassion, they contribute to the development of a thriving educational community where all members can flourish and reach their full potential, benefiting both teachers and students alike.

What Does It Mean to Embody Compassion as a School Leader?

Effective leadership is not merely about making decisions and implementing policies; it's about creating an environment where compassion thrives. Compassionate leadership is an approach that places human connection at its core, with active listening, empathy, support, inclusivity, and transparency as its cornerstones. In this section, we explore these five essential qualities, beginning with active listening, which forms the foundation for compassionate leadership.

◆ **Active Listening:** Active listening is the bedrock upon which compassionate leadership is built. It involves not merely hearing but truly understanding the concerns, ideas, and emotions of others. When school leaders embrace active listening, they create a space where every voice is valued. By engaging in active listening, leaders can build trust, make informed decisions, and foster a sense of being heard and valued within the school community.

◆ **Empathy:** Empathy is the bridge that allows school leaders to connect with the experiences and emotions of students, staff, and parents. It goes beyond sympathy; it is the ability to put oneself in another's shoes and understand their perspective deeply. Empathetic leaders respond with sensitivity and understanding, a crucial aspect of building positive relationships and addressing individual needs effectively.

◆ **Supportive and Encouraging:** Providing unwavering support and encouragement demonstrates a leader's commitment to the growth and well-being of their team members and students. This quality creates an environment where motivation and empowerment flourish. It inspires individuals to reach their full potential and contribute to the school's success, knowing that their leader is behind them every step of the way.

◆ **Inclusivity:** Creating an inclusive environment is an imperative aspect of compassionate leadership. Inclusivity ensures that all members of the school community feel valued and respected, regardless of their background or differences. Compassionate leaders actively promote diversity and work tirelessly to eliminate bias and discrimination, thus contributing to a harmonious and equitable school culture where everyone has the opportunity to thrive.

◆ **Transparency:** Transparency in communication and decision-making is the cornerstone of trust and credibility. Compassionate leaders do not operate in the shadows; they share their actions, provide clear explanations, and involve others in the decision-making process when appropriate. Transparency fosters a sense of openness and accountability within the school community, ensuring that everyone is informed and confident in the leadership's intentions and actions.

Strategies to Develop Compassionate Skills

Compassion involves understanding and empathizing with the challenges, needs, and emotions of others. In the context of school leadership, compassion plays a pivotal role in nurturing a positive and supportive educational environment. By developing compassion as a school leader, you can create a nurturing and inclusive atmosphere where teachers, students, and the community can flourish and reach their full potential.

◆ **Compassion Cultivation Practices:** Engaging in compassion cultivation practices and role-playing activities helps leaders practice stepping into the perspectives of others and responding with compassion. This skill is critical for connecting with students, staff, and parents and is at the heart of compassionate leadership. For instance, a school principal practices mindfulness to better understand and support students facing personal difficulties, creating a more trusting and inclusive school community.

◆ **Feedback and Self-Assessment:** Regularly seeking feedback from colleagues, subordinates, and stakeholders is essential for assessing and improving compassionate leadership skills. Constructive feedback helps leaders identify areas for growth and adapt their approach accordingly. A school leader who actively solicits feedback from teachers and parents can adapt their approach to create a more compassionate and effective educational environment.

◆ **Mentorship and Coaching:** Learning from experienced leaders known for their compassionate leadership style can be highly beneficial. Mentorship and coaching allows you to learn from someone who embodies compassion in their leadership approach. Seeking mentorship from such a leader provides personalized guidance, helping a school leader become a role model for compassionate leadership.

◆ **Setting Clear Compassion Goals:** Establishing specific goals for practicing empathetic leadership is crucial. These goals could include fostering a more inclusive environment, improving communication, or enhancing the overall well-being of the school community. For example, a department head sets a goal to create a more inclusive environment for students with diverse backgrounds, leading to initiatives that foster inclusivity.

◆ **Practice Empathetic Leadership:** Integrating empathy into everyday leadership practices is essential. Leaders who actively demonstrate empathy in their interactions with students, staff, and parents can create a more inclusive and supportive school culture. For example, a superintendent who actively practices empathetic leadership through open and compassionate dialogues with teachers and parents fosters an environment where everyone's voice is valued.

◆ **Leading by Example:** Your conduct is meticulously observed and often emulated by others. Demonstrating compassion through your actions is a potent means to exert a positive influence on your community. Its significance is evident in the ensuing aspects:

◆ **Inspiring Compassionate Behavior:** Consistently exemplifying compassion in your interactions serves as an inspiration for others to follow suit. Your behavior sets the standard for the entire school community.

◆ **Supporting Staff:** Expressing gratitude for your staff, commemorating their accomplishments, and offering assistance when required instills a culture of recognition and encouragement. This, in turn, elevates morale and job satisfaction among teachers and staff.

As we leave this section, here are five examples that you can implement right away:

1. **Morning Greetings and Check-Ins:** As a school leader, you can start the day by personally greeting your teachers and staff members as they arrive at school. Take a moment to ask about their well-being and any challenges they may be facing. This simple act of showing genuine interest and empathy sets a positive tone for the day and lets your team know you care about their welfare. Also, when you visit classrooms, leave a post-it note on their desk telling them how lucky their students are to have them and share something you learned or enjoyed about the visit. I call them **"Post-its of Praise"**!

2. **Supporting Teachers' Professional Development:** Compassionate leadership involves investing in the growth of your teachers. Allocate resources and time for professional development opportunities, workshops, and training sessions. Encourage teachers to pursue advanced degrees or certifications and provide financial support or incentives for their efforts.

3. **Active Listening During Meetings:** During staff meetings or one-on-one discussions, practice active listening. Give your full attention to the speaker, maintain eye contact, and refrain from interrupting. Encourage teachers and staff to share their ideas, concerns, and feedback openly. Acknowledge their contributions and express gratitude for their dedication.

4. **Acknowledging Achievements and Milestones:** Celebrate the accomplishments of your school community, both big and small. Recognize teachers, students, and staff for their hard work, achievements, and contributions. Host regular appreciation events, awards ceremonies, or newsletters that highlight success stories and positive outcomes.

5. **Inclusive Decision-Making:** Involve teachers and staff in the decision-making process whenever possible. Seek their input on matters related to curriculum development, school policies, and resource allocation. This collaborative approach empowers your team and fosters a sense of ownership and trust.

The Benefits of Compassion in School Leadership

Compassionate leadership shapes not only the policies and practices but also the very culture of a school, from the creation of an enriched school culture to the nurturing of teacher morale, and from driving positive school outcomes to ensuring long-term sustainability, compassionate leadership serves as a basis of excellence in education.

◆ **Enhanced School Culture:** Compassionate leadership plays a pivotal role in creating an enhanced school culture. When leaders prioritize compassion, they set an example for everyone in the school community. This results in an atmosphere where mutual respect, understanding, and empathy prevail. A positive school culture not only makes students feel safe and welcomed but also encourages teachers and staff to collaborate and innovate.

Example: *A principal who demonstrates compassion by actively listening to teachers' concerns, acknowledging their hard work, and involving them in decision-making fosters a school culture where open communication and collaboration thrive. This, in turn, leads to a more cohesive and harmonious educational environment.*

◆ **Improved Teacher Morale:** Compassionate leaders prioritize the well-being of their teachers and staff, which directly impacts morale. When educators feel valued, supported, and heard, they are more motivated to excel in their roles. This improved morale translates into better teaching quality, increased job satisfaction, and reduced turnover rates.

Example: *A superintendent who regularly meets with teachers, listens to their feedback, and provides resources to address their needs shows compassion. As a result, teachers are more enthusiastic about their work, leading to improved student outcomes and a more positive school atmosphere.*

◆ **Positive School Outcomes:** Compassionate leadership contributes to positive school outcomes in various ways. When students, teachers, and staff feel cared for and supported, academic performance tends to improve. Additionally, compassionate leaders are more likely to implement policies and practices that prioritize student success and personal growth.

Example: *A compassionate principal actively involves parents in their child's education, making them feel part of the school community. This inclusive approach can lead to higher student attendance, increased parental involvement, and ultimately, improved academic outcomes.*

◆ **Long-Term Sustainability:** Compassionate leaders focus on building a strong foundation for the long-term sustainability of the school. By nurturing relationships, fostering a positive culture, and making ethical decisions, they ensure the school's ability to adapt to changing circumstances, economic challenges, and evolving educational needs.

Example: *A compassionate school board allocates resources wisely, ensuring that funding is directed toward programs and initiatives that benefit students and the community. This prudent financial management helps secure the school's long-term sustainability.*

◆ **Reduced Stress and Personal Fulfillment:** Compassionate leaders prioritize the well-being of their team members and recognize the importance of work–life balance. By promoting a healthy and supportive work environment, they reduce stress and burnout among teachers and staff. This, in turn, leads to better mental and physical health and greater personal fulfillment in their roles.

Example: *A compassionate school principal encourages teachers to take regular breaks, attend professional development opportunities, and maintain a work–life balance. This leads to reduced stress levels among staff and a more motivated and fulfilled teaching staff, resulting in a positive impact on student learning.*

Utilizing Your Compassionate Edge

A compassionate leader understands the importance of connecting with their team, students, parents, and stakeholders on a human level, recognizing that each individual brings their unique perspectives and concerns to the table. This compassion, this ability to empathize and act with genuine concern for the well-being of others, is what gives a leader an essential edge in guiding a school towards success and harmonious growth. Let's examine five key scenarios, each with its unique challenges and opportunities for compassion in leadership.

1. Faculty Meetings:
   - Situation: Leading a faculty meeting with differing opinions and ideas.
   - Action: Approach faculty meetings with an emphasis on respecting diverse viewpoints and emotions. Show

empathy by acknowledging their contributions and concerns. Encourage a culture of respect and inclusion in meetings, ensuring everyone's voice is heard.

2. Parent-Teacher Conferences:
   - Situation: Meeting with parents who may have concerns or demands.
   - Action: Approach parent-teacher conferences with a genuine desire to understand parents' worries and needs. Offer emotional support when addressing their concerns and reassure them of your commitment to their child's well-being and academic success.

3. Discipline Issues:
   - Situation: Addressing student discipline issues with parents and teachers.
   - Action: Approach disciplinary issues with a focus on rehabilitation and growth rather than punitive measures. Offer counseling and support to students and collaborate with parents and teachers to create a supportive environment for the student's improvement.

4. Implementing Changes:
   - Situation: Introducing new policies, procedures, or educational initiatives.
   - Action: When introducing changes, engage in transparent and empathetic communication with all stakeholders. Address concerns with patience and understanding, offering support and resources to those affected by the changes.

5. Seeking Support from Superiors:
   - Situation: Advocating for additional resources or support from higher-ups.
   - Action: Advocate for additional support while considering the broader impact on the school community. Emphasize how the requested resources will benefit not only the institution but also the students and staff.

7

Navigating Conflict with Balanced Leadership

Erin Brockovich, portrayed by Julia Roberts in the movie *Erin Brockovich* (2000), offers a compelling example of a leader who deftly balanced assertiveness and compassion while addressing a complex conflict. Her assertiveness was evident in her meticulous investigation of environmental contamination caused by a utility company. Erin collected substantial evidence to support her case, setting clear expectations that the company must take responsibility for its actions. She embraced open dialogue by engaging affected community members and empowering them to voice their concerns. Erin's assertiveness was instrumental in advocating for justice on behalf of the community.

Complementing her assertiveness was Erin's profound compassion for the community members suffering from environmental contamination. She demonstrated deep empathy by actively listening to their emotions and perspectives. Erin provided unwavering emotional support, acknowledging the difficulties they faced and prioritizing their well-being. Her compassion extended beyond the legal battle, addressing the emotional needs of the community. Erin's commitment to their welfare was a driving force behind her tireless pursuit of justice.

Erin Brockovich's remarkable ability to balance compassion with assertiveness in addressing the environmental conflict is a key aspect of her leadership. Her empathy and emotional support

DOI: 10.4324/9781032657745-8

for the community members didn't undermine her assertive advocacy; they strengthened it by grounding it in a deep sense of purpose and care.

As a school leader, you can draw significant takeaways from her approach to conflict resolution, understanding that compassion can enhance assertiveness, making it more effective and purpose-driven. This balanced approach can lead to more meaningful and impactful conflict resolution, fostering trust and unity within the school community. You should prioritize empathy, emotional support, and the well-being of their students and community members when addressing conflicts, using these qualities to guide their assertive actions. This approach can create a positive and inclusive school environment where conflicts are resolved with care and determination, ultimately benefitting the entire school community.

Conflict: Neither Good nor Bad, but How It's Handled Matters

Conflict is a fundamental aspect of human interactions, arising from the diversity of opinions, needs, and interests that characterize our relationships and societies. It can be likened to a double-edged sword, with both negative and positive facets, depending on how it is approached and managed. In educational settings, some educators may tend to perceive conflict as inherently bad, particularly those who are high in agreeableness, due to its potential disruption to the learning environment and its emotional toll, leading them to avoid it, often missing out on valuable teaching moments and opportunities for growth.

Negative Aspects of Conflict
- ◆ **Escalation:** Conflict can take a negative turn when it escalates beyond a healthy discourse. When disagreements evolve into hostility and aggression, they can inflict emotional wounds and irreparable harm on relationships. Unchecked escalation can lead to destructive confrontations.

◆ **Destructive Communication:** Poorly managed conflicts often involve hurtful or disrespectful communication. Words and actions during conflict can leave lasting scars, damaging not only the immediate relationship but also the individuals involved. This type of communication can erode trust and respect.

◆ **Stress and Anxiety:** Conflict, when left unresolved or mishandled, can be a significant source of stress and anxiety. The constant tension and uncertainty that accompany ongoing disputes can take a toll on mental and physical health, impacting overall well-being.

◆ **Damage to Relationships:** Perhaps the most evident negative consequence of mishandled conflict is the damage it inflicts on relationships. When conflict is not addressed constructively, it can result in bitterness, grudges, and strained connections, sometimes leading to permanent rifts between individuals or groups.

Positive Aspects of Conflict

◆ **Problem-Solving:** Conflict can serve as a catalyst for problem-solving and innovation. When individuals or groups encounter differences in perspectives or interests, they may be motivated to find creative solutions to address these challenges, leading to improved outcomes.

◆ **Improved Understanding:** Conflict forces parties involved to listen, empathize, and learn from each other's perspectives. Through this process, individuals can gain a deeper understanding of each other's needs and motivations, potentially fostering empathy and reducing prejudice.

◆ **Growth and Development:** Managing and resolving conflict can lead to personal and interpersonal growth. Individuals who engage in effective conflict resolution develop better communication and negotiation skills, which are valuable in various aspects of life.

◆ **Strengthening Relationships:** When conflict is addressed constructively, it can demonstrate that parties are willing to work together to overcome challenges. Successfully navigating conflict can strengthen relationships by building trust and highlighting the resilience of the bond between individuals or groups.

Remember, conflict itself is neither inherently negative nor positive. Its outcome depends on how it is approached and managed. By employing effective conflict resolution techniques such as active listening, compromise, and open communication, individuals and groups can transform potential sources of negativity into opportunities for growth, understanding, and relationship strengthening.

The Role of Assertiveness in Conflict Resolution

Assertiveness is a critical skill for you as a school leader in addressing conflicts effectively. It allows you to communicate your concerns and expectations clearly while maintaining boundaries, ensuring that conflicts are resolved in a timely and constructive manner. For example, when a teacher expresses dissatisfaction with a new school policy, your assertiveness enables you to address their concerns directly and work toward a resolution.

◆ **The Power of Assertive Communication:** Assertive communication is the foundation of effective conflict resolution. It involves confidently and respectfully expressing thoughts, needs, or concerns. In conflict resolution, assertiveness ensures that concerns and expectations are conveyed clearly, reducing misunderstandings and expediting resolution. When you use assertive communication, you create an environment where conflicts can be addressed promptly, preventing issues from festering or escalating unnecessarily.

◆ **Open and Direct Communication:** Open and direct communication is a fundamental component of assertiveness. It entails discussing concerns or grievances in a respectful and non-confrontational manner. Using strategies like "I" statements to express feelings and thoughts fosters an environment conducive to open dialogue. For instance, when addressing a parent's concerns about a disciplinary matter, you actively listen without interruption, ensuring a complete understanding of the situation.

◆ **Setting Clear Boundaries:** Setting clear boundaries is a critical aspect of assertive conflict resolution. It involves establishing explicit guidelines that define acceptable behavior and expectations. Clear boundaries contribute to a structured and orderly conflict resolution process, minimizing the potential for disputes. By setting and upholding clear boundaries, you signal your commitment to a fair and transparent conflict resolution process.

◆ **Dealing with Low Agreeableness:** Individuals Encounters with individuals displaying low agreeableness traits are not uncommon in school leadership. These individuals often exhibit confrontational behavior during conflicts, expressing strong opposition or resistance to change. It is essential to recognize this behavior and employ assertive communication strategies to address their concerns effectively.

Identifying individuals with low agreeableness traits is the first step. They may frequently challenge policies, question decisions, or resist change. Assertive communication empowers you to engage in constructive dialogue while maintaining professionalism and fairness. Maintaining composure, active listening, and validating concerns can help de-escalate confrontations and guide discussions toward resolution.

For example, a low agreeableness teacher might consistently oppose changes in curriculum, classroom policies, or school initiatives without considering alternative viewpoints. Managing conflicts with such teachers often requires assertive communication and conflict resolution strategies to address their concerns effectively. Offering constructive feedback, emphasizing common goals, and considering mediation when conflicts persist are additional strategies for effective conflict management.

Strategies for Handling Low Agreeableness Individuals

♦ **Maintaining Calm and Composure:** Strive to remain composed and level-headed when interacting with individuals exhibiting low agreeableness. For instance, when a parent strongly opposes a change in school policy, respond calmly and professionally to avoid escalating emotions.

♦ **Active Listening and Validating Concerns:** Actively listen to the concerns and opinions of low agreeableness individuals without interrupting or judging. Demonstrate genuine interest in understanding their perspective. For example, if a teacher expresses strong opposition to a new teaching methodology, acknowledge their concerns and validate their feelings.

♦ **Offering Constructive Feedback:** When addressing concerns with low agreeableness individuals, provide specific and actionable feedback. Explain how your approach aligns with best practices and the school's values. For instance, if a parent disagrees with the school's discipline approach, offer constructive feedback to foster a more productive dialogue.

♦ **Focusing on Solutions and Common Goals:** Steer discussions toward finding common ground and identifying potential solutions. Emphasize shared goals and collaborate to reach agreements. For example, if a teacher opposes changes to the curriculum, work together to find a curriculum that meets both their concerns and educational objectives.

♦ **Exploring Compromise and Collaboration:** Demonstrate flexibility by being open to compromise while upholding essential boundaries. For instance, if parents oppose a school schedule change, explore compromise by adjusting the schedule to accommodate certain concerns.

♦ **Consideration of Mediation or Third-Party Involvement:** When conflicts with low agreeableness individuals persist, consider involving a mediator or third party to facilitate resolution. For example, if a dispute between parents and the school administration remains unresolved, the involvement of a neutral mediator can help both parties reach a mutually agreeable resolution.

Implementing these strategies empowers you to effectively manage conflicts with individuals displaying low agreeableness traits, fostering constructive dialogue and maintaining a positive school environment.

The Role of Compassion in Conflict Resolution

Compassion and Active Listening

Compassion and active listening are pivotal qualities for you in conflict resolution. Compassion involves understanding and addressing the emotions and perspectives of those involved in conflicts, while active listening is the skill of fully engaging with what others are saying, showing empathy and openness. These qualities create an environment where individuals feel valued and heard during conflict resolution discussions. For instance, you actively listen to a teacher who is upset about a change in the school's grading policy, demonstrating empathy and understanding, allowing the teacher to express their concerns fully.

In your compassionate approach to conflict resolution, you go beyond surface issues and focus on understanding and empathizing with the emotions and perspectives of those involved. It involves addressing conflicts by taking into account the feelings and needs of individuals in conflict. This approach can build trust, strengthen relationships, and lead to more constructive outcomes in conflicts. For example, you resolve a conflict among two students who have been arguing by taking the time to understand the reasons behind their disagreement and finding a solution that satisfies both parties.

Creating a safe and supportive environment in the context of conflict resolution is essential for you as a school leader. It involves building trust and ensuring confidentiality for individuals addressing conflicts. Trust is established through consistent and fair conflict resolution processes, while confidentiality ensures that individuals can express concerns without fear of repercussions. This environment encourages open and honest communication during conflict resolution discussions and allows individuals to feel safe and heard. For instance, you ensure that during staff meetings, teachers can openly discuss their concerns, knowing that their input will remain confidential, fostering trust and open communication.

Handling conflict-averse teachers involves recognizing the challenges posed by educators who tend to avoid confrontation and express concerns indirectly. Conflict-averse teachers may prefer one-on-one discussions to avoid potential conflict within group dynamics or staff meetings. You need to adapt your conflict resolution strategies accordingly, understanding the preferences and tendencies of these teachers. For example, in a staff meeting, a high-agreeableness teacher indirectly expresses concerns about a new teaching method, preferring private discussions to avoid potential conflict within the group.

Balancing compassion with assertiveness in conflict resolution is crucial for you as a school leader. It means finding the equilibrium between showing empathy and maintaining boundaries. You must discern when to express understanding and when to assert expectations or boundaries firmly, depending on the specific circumstances and individuals involved in the conflict. For instance, when addressing a teacher's repeated classroom management issues, you could listen empathetically to their reasoning before agreeing on an action plan for success.

Your strategies for effective conflict resolution encompass various techniques and approaches, such as active listening, providing constructive feedback, emphasizing collaboration, offering conflict resolution training, and considering mediation when conflicts persist. These strategies equip you with the necessary skills to navigate conflicts successfully and promote positive outcomes. For example, you facilitate collaboration between two teachers with differing teaching approaches, helping them find common ground and improve their teaching methods through constructive feedback and collaboration.

Effective conflict resolution for you as relies on a delicate balance of compassion, active listening, assertiveness, and fostering a safe and supportive environment. Compassion and active listening create understanding and open communication, while a compassionate approach focuses on emotions and perspectives, leading to constructive outcomes. Building trust and adapting to conflict-averse teachers' tendencies are crucial. Balancing compassion with assertiveness means *knowing when to express empathy and when to assert expectations*. Employing various conflict resolution strategies equips you with the skills to navigate conflicts successfully, enhancing the educational experience and the school community's overall success.

The Power of Face-to-Face Conversations in Resolving Conflict

As school leaders, your role extends far beyond administrative duties and curriculum planning. You are entrusted with creating a positive and harmonious environment for both your staff and students. Conflict is an inevitable part of any organization, but how you handle it can make all the difference. While emails, written communication, and staff meetings have their place, there are times when tough conversations need to happen face-to-face. In this section, we will discuss the importance of personal, one-on-one discussions when dealing with conflicts within your school community.

◆ **The Impact of Face-to-Face Communication:** Face-to-face conversations are a powerful tool for addressing conflicts within your school. Here's why they matter:
  • **Builds Trust:** Meeting in person shows that you care about the issue and the person involved. It builds trust and fosters a sense of connection that emails simply cannot achieve.
  • **Clearer Communication:** In face-to-face interactions, you can pick up on non-verbal cues such as

body language and tone of voice. This enhances understanding and reduces misinterpretation.

- **Immediate Resolution:** Emails can often lead to back-and-forth exchanges that prolong the conflict. Face-to-face conversations allow you to address the issue directly, leading to quicker resolutions.

◆ **When to Choose Face-to-Face Conversations:** While email and other written forms of communication have their merits, there are situations where you should consider having a face-to-face conversation:

- **Sensitive Issues:** When dealing with highly sensitive or emotional topics, such as personal conflicts among staff members or disciplinary matters, a face-to-face discussion is often more appropriate.
- **Complex Problems:** For complex issues that require detailed explanations, brainstorming, or negotiation, in-person discussions provide a more effective platform.
- **Relationship Preservation:** When conflicts risk damaging relationships, meeting in person shows your commitment to resolving the issue while maintaining a positive connection.

◆ **Preparing for Tough Conversations:** Before initiating a face-to-face conversation to address a conflict, consider these steps:

- **Gather Information:** Collect all relevant facts and data to ensure a well-informed discussion.
- **Choose the Right Time and Place:** Find a neutral and private setting where both parties can talk openly without distractions.
- **Practice Active Listening:** Be prepared to listen actively, ask open-ended questions, and seek to understand the other person's perspective.
- **Stay Calm and Professional:** Emotions can run high during tough conversations. Maintain composure, stay respectful, and avoid confrontational language.

◆ **Follow-Up and Resolution:** After the face-to-face conversation, it's important to follow up and ensure that the agreed-upon solutions or actions are carried out. This demonstrates your commitment to resolution and can help prevent future conflicts.

We understand that face-to-face meetings to address conflicts can be uncomfortable, and at times, you may wish to avoid them. However, it's essential to recognize that not having these conversations can have a significant impact on the morale and well-being of everyone within your school community.

Educational settings are particularly sensitive to this discomfort due to the agreeable nature often found among teachers. They may grapple with feelings of guilt even when conflicts are addressed through email or meetings, even if they had no involvement.

This tendency to internalize conflicts, combined with the altruistic nature of educators, can lead to several adverse outcomes. When conflicts are left unresolved or are only dealt with through emails or staff meetings, it can result in confusion and frustration among staff members. Questions may arise about why certain issues remain unaddressed or why some individuals appear to receive preferential treatment, eroding trust within the school community and fostering doubt and uncertainty.

Ultimately, this erosion of trust and teamwork directly impacts overall morale within the school. When colleagues are unsure about how conflicts are handled or feel that their voices are not heard, it can create a negative atmosphere that hinders collaboration and diminishes enthusiasm.

While face-to-face conversations may be uncomfortable, avoiding them can result in a chain reaction of negative consequences, affecting individuals involved in conflicts and the broader school community. Recognizing and addressing this discomfort is crucial for nurturing a healthier, more harmonious school environment where conflicts are effectively resolved, trust is reinforced, and morale remains high.

Strategies for Developing a Balanced Approach

Developing assertiveness as a school leader takes practice and self-awareness. Here are some strategies to help school leaders become more assertive in conflict resolution:

◆ **Self-Reflection:** Taking time for self-reflection involves examining your own values, beliefs, and boundaries. By doing so, you become more self-aware, which in turn helps you articulate your concerns and expectations more effectively. For example, you might reflect on your personal values of fairness and inclusivity, which informs your approach to resolving conflicts involving students.

◆ **Effective Communication:** Enhancing communication skills is crucial. Practice active listening, which means fully engaging with what others are saying, avoiding interruptions or judgment, and focusing on the issue at hand. For instance, during a conversation with a parent regarding a disciplinary matter, you actively listen to the parent's concerns without interruption, ensuring you fully understand the situation.

◆ **Conflict Resolution Training:** Attending conflict resolution workshops or training sessions exposes you to new techniques and strategies for assertive communication. By learning and applying these skills, you become better equipped to address conflicts. For example, participating in a conflict resolution training program teaches you how to use "I" statements effectively during disagreements with teachers or staff.

◆ **Seek Feedback:** Actively seek feedback from colleagues, staff members, or mentors to gain insights into your assertiveness skills and areas for improvement. For instance, you may request feedback from your team after resolving a challenging conflict to understand how you can enhance your approach.

◆ **Practice Empathy:** Cultivating empathy involves putting yourself in the shoes of others to understand their perspectives and emotions. This skill helps you respond with empathy and understanding during conflicts. For example, when addressing a student's behavioral issues, you consider the student's background and experiences to better understand their behavior.

◆ **Cultivate Active Listening Skills:** Actively listening means being fully present and engaged in conversations. Avoid interrupting or judging and instead, create a safe space for open dialogue. During a meeting with teachers discussing curriculum changes, you practice active listening by giving your full attention to each teacher's input, ensuring that all voices are heard.

◆ **Promote a Supportive Environment:** You play a vital role in creating an atmosphere where individuals feel comfortable expressing their concerns and opinions. You encourage open dialogue and respect diverse viewpoints. For example, you foster a supportive environment by holding regular staff meetings where teachers can openly share their ideas and concerns without fear of retribution.

◆ **Positive Outcomes:** Remember conflict is not inherently good or bad, so when it is managed effectively in school leadership, it yields multiple positive outcomes. It serves as a platform for innovative problem-solving, allowing diverse perspectives to converge into creative solutions for educational challenges. Furthermore, constructive conflict resolution promotes transparent and open communication among stakeholders, nurturing a culture of understanding within the school community. This, in turn, strengthens relationships and fosters mutual respect among students, teachers, parents, and staff members. Conflict resolution skills developed during these processes also contribute to personal and professional growth, enhancing negotiation, active listening, empathy, and problem-solving capabilities. These skills can prove valuable across various aspects of school leadership and staff roles. Additionally, addressing conflicts constructively enables adaptation to changing educational landscapes, promoting innovation in teaching methods, policies, and practices. Ultimately, it builds trust among stakeholders, reinforcing the leadership's commitment to fairness and the well-being of the school community. This trust, combined with the unity nurtured through conflict resolution, cultivates a more harmonious and successful educational environment.

Remember, finding the right balance between assertiveness and compassion is essential when navigating conflict as a school leader. It requires understanding when to be firm and assertive, and when to show empathy and understanding.

So, start by addressing the issue assertively, clearly expressing your concerns and expectations. This sets the foundation for open and honest communication. Then, transition into a more compassionate approach by actively listening to the perspectives and feelings of others. This helps create a safe space for collaborative problem-solving and resolution.

Remember, finding the balance between assertiveness and compassion is not about compromising your values or boundaries. It is about creating an environment where conflicts can be resolved effectively while maintaining positive relationships.

The Competitive Edge of Effective Conflict Management

Conflict is an inherent part of human interactions, and how it's managed is crucial in school leadership. Effective conflict management provides school leaders with a significant edge in their effectiveness. Addressing conflicts assertively and compassionately through face-to-face conversations fosters trust, reduces misunderstandings, and leads to quicker resolutions. Trust is vital in educational settings where relationships between staff, students, parents, and administrators are key to a productive school community.

Moreover, combining assertiveness with compassion in conflict resolution yields positive outcomes, including innovative problem-solving, transparent communication, and personal and professional growth. These skills enhance the effectiveness of school leaders and staff in various roles. Creating a supportive environment where individuals feel safe expressing concerns promotes understanding and unity within the school community. Conflict resolution skills honed in this context contribute to better negotiation, active listening, empathy, and problem-solving abilities, essential in school leadership.

Lastly, effectively addressing conflicts allows the school environment to adapt to the changing educational landscape by encouraging innovation in teaching methods, policies, and practices. This reinforces trust among stakeholders, reaffirming the leadership's commitment to fairness and the school community's well-being. This trust, combined with unity nurtured through conflict resolution, cultivates a harmonious and successful educational environment. In essence, mastering the balance between assertiveness and compassion gives school leaders a competitive edge in leadership effectiveness, creating a thriving educational environment for all stakeholders.

8

Empowering and Motivating Staff

Lee Iacocca is one of my favorite leaders because of his incredible success in revitalizing struggling organizations. He exemplifies the qualities of a servant leader by focusing on the empowerment and well-being of his staff, demonstrating that effective leadership can drive transformative results.

In the early 1980s, Chrysler Corporation faced a financial crisis, declining market share, and low employee morale, akin to challenges in education. When Lee Iacocca became CEO in 1978, he demonstrated how empowering and motivating staff could drive significant change. He empowered employees by encouraging their input and innovations, much like school leaders foster an environment where educators feel valued and encouraged to share their insights.

Iacocca's unique move was putting workers on the board, giving them a voice in decision-making – a practice akin to involving teachers and staff in school governance. He rallied employees around a common vision, a strategy school leaders often employ to unite their teams for educational success.

Iacocca's leadership, exemplified by leading by example and transparent communication, built trust among employees. Similarly, in education, open, honest communication and trust are vital to creating a positive and collaborative school environment.

Lee Iacocca's transformational leadership at Chrysler serves as an inspiring example of how empowering and motivating

DOI: 10.4324/9781032657745-9

staff, including giving them a role in decision-making, can lead to remarkable turnarounds, even in the face of adversity. You can draw inspiration from Iacocca's leadership style, emphasizing empowerment, motivation, and trust-building, to drive positive change in your schools.

Empowering staff goes beyond just assigning tasks and giving instructions. It involves providing employees with the autonomy and authority to make decisions and take ownership of their work. When employees feel empowered, they become more engaged in their roles. They feel a sense of responsibility and are motivated to perform at their best. This increased engagement leads to higher productivity levels and better overall job satisfaction.

For example, imagine a school where teachers are given the freedom to design their own lesson plans and choose teaching methods that they believe will be most effective for their students. This empowerment allows teachers to tap into their creativity and expertise, resulting in engaging and impactful lessons. As a result, students become more enthusiastic about learning, leading to improved academic performance and increased student outcomes.

◆ **Enhanced Collaboration:** Empowered individuals are more likely to collaborate effectively, as they have the confidence and trust in their abilities to contribute meaningfully to a team. When staff members feel empowered, they are more willing to share their ideas, experiences, and knowledge, leading to enhanced collaboration and synergy within the organization.

   For example: *In a healthcare setting, empowering nurses to make decisions regarding patient care can greatly improve collaboration among the healthcare team. When nurses are empowered to voice their opinions and suggestions, they can provide valuable insights and contribute to better patient outcomes. This collaboration and teamwork results in a more efficient and effective healthcare delivery system.*

◆ **Student Outcomes:** Empowering staff members has a direct impact on student outcomes. When teachers and other educational staff members feel empowered, they are more motivated to create a positive learning environment where students can thrive. Empowered staff members are more likely to go the extra mile to support their students, provide personalized attention, and respond to their unique needs.

    For example: *In a school where teachers are empowered to tailor their teaching methods to meet the individual needs of each student, students are more likely to receive the support they require to succeed academically. This personalized approach to education leads to improved student outcomes, such as higher graduation rates, increased student engagement, and better academic performance.*

◆ **Open Communication:** Establishing open and transparent communication channels is crucial for sustaining empowerment within an organization. When staff members feel comfortable expressing their ideas, concerns, and suggestions, it fosters a culture of trust, collaboration, and innovation.

    For example: *Implementing meetings where staff members are encouraged to share their thoughts and opinions can improve communication within the school. Additionally, creating platforms for anonymous feedback can further enhance open communication, as it allows staff members to express their concerns without fear of retribution. This open communication culture creates a supportive environment where staff members can freely contribute their ideas, leading to continuous improvement and growth for the organization as a whole.*

Empowering staff members is crucial for boosting engagement, enhancing collaboration, improving student outcomes, and establishing open communication within an organization. By providing employees with autonomy, authority, and the resources they need to succeed, organizations can create a positive work environment that fosters innovation, creativity, and growth. Empowered staff members are more motivated, engaged, and committed, resulting in improved performance and overall success for the organization.

The Importance of Empowering and Motivating Teachers/Staff

The empowerment and motivation of teachers and staff are vital components in the success of educational institutions. This is particularly crucial given the common sentiment among educators that their voices often go unheard, and their invaluable contributions are sometimes undervalued, despite the pivotal role they play.

When teachers and staff are empowered, they develop a profound sense of ownership and responsibility within the educational institution. This empowerment encourages them to take proactive steps, make informed decisions, and actively contribute to the ongoing growth and enhancement of the school. Consequently, this heightened sense of empowerment leads to increased job satisfaction and a deepened commitment to their profession.

Within an environment that prioritizes motivation and empowerment, educators are more inclined to collaborate and exchange ideas with their colleagues. This collaborative spirit fosters a culture of continuous learning and professional development, which ultimately benefits students. Motivated educators are more likely to embrace innovative teaching practices, adapt to evolving pedagogical approaches, and stay informed about the latest educational research, ensuring the constant improvement of their teaching methods.

The impact of motivated educators on student outcomes cannot be overstated. Motivated teachers often go the extra mile for their students, providing personalized attention and unwavering support. They are dedicated to addressing the unique needs of each student, ensuring that no one is left behind. This personalized approach results in increased student engagement and higher levels of academic achievement.

Furthermore, motivated teachers significantly contribute to shaping the overall school culture. Their enthusiasm and passion for teaching serve as an inspiration to students, motivating them to actively engage in their own educational journeys. Students are more likely to develop a genuine love for learning when they witness the dedication and commitment of their teachers.

Beyond the direct impact on student outcomes, the empowerment and motivation of teachers and staff also play a pivotal role in the overall success of the educational institution. A positive work environment not only attracts talented educators but also retains them, resulting in a stable and experienced teaching staff. This stability, in turn, fosters a sense of continuity and consistency for students, enhancing their overall educational experience.

By cultivating a positive and collaborative work environment, educators become more inclined to embrace innovative teaching practices, provide individualized attention to students, and exert a positive influence on student outcomes. Empowering and motivating teachers not only benefits the students but also contributes to the overarching success and culture of the educational institution.

Understanding the Needs and Challenges of Teachers/Staff

Understanding the needs and challenges of teachers and staff is a foundational step for school leaders in building an environment that fosters empowerment and motivation among educators. It is imperative for school leaders to recognize the distinct requirements and obstacles faced by their teaching staff. To achieve this, school leaders can implement several strategies.

To foster open and honest communication within the school community, leaders should prioritize individual interactions over group staff meetings. Encouraging teachers to freely express their thoughts, concerns, and ideas in a one-on-one setting allows leaders to gain valuable insights into what motivates and hinders each educator personally. For example, instead of relying solely on large staff meetings, school leaders should schedule regular individual check-ins with teachers. These confidential interactions provide educators with a more personalized opportunity to share their experiences and concerns. For instance, a monthly one-on-one meeting with each teacher enables school leaders to address specific issues, offer tailored support, and build a deeper understanding of individual needs and aspirations.

In these individual meetings, school leaders can adopt a more proactive approach, which I call *aspirational conversations*, by asking five key questions that focus on empowerment and professional growth:

1. Have we helped you succeed?
2. What do you think we do well, such as reading programs, extracurricular activities, etc.?
3. What improvements or practices have you observed in other schools that you believe could benefit our institution?
4. What conditions or factors might make you consider leaving our school?
5. What are your professional goals, and how can we support you in achieving them?

These questions shift the conversation towards an aspirational and growth-oriented approach. School leaders can emphasize their commitment to helping teachers succeed, acknowledging their strengths, and addressing areas for improvement. By showing a genuine interest in teachers' professional development and career goals, leaders demonstrate that they value their educators and are willing to invest in their growth, ultimately fostering a culture of empowerment and motivation. Importantly, as previously emphasized, leaders should remain receptive without passing judgment; by refraining, for instance, from taking feedback personally.

Surveys and feedback mechanisms can also be employed to gather insights from teachers and staff. These tools can assess job satisfaction, gauge opinions on school policies, and identify areas that require additional support. For instance, anonymous surveys can uncover whether educators feel valued and empowered in their roles and pinpoint specific challenges that need attention.

Moreover, school leaders should actively involve teachers and staff in decision-making processes. This approach empowers educators and ensures that decisions align with their needs and concerns. For example, when contemplating changes in curriculum or teaching methods, leaders can seek input from educators who are directly involved, as they possess valuable insights based on their experiences.

Creating a safe and nurturing environment in which teachers can freely express their opinions and experiences without apprehension of negative consequences is of paramount importance. It is essential for school leaders to avoid adopting an aggressive leadership style that perceives any form of dissent as a personal attack. Most teachers are deeply committed to their profession and may already be hesitant to voice concerns, so fostering an atmosphere of open dialogue is crucial to alleviate these fears. When educators feel respected and recognized as professionals, their engagement and motivation naturally thrive, ultimately enhancing the overall quality and productivity of the educational environment.

Fostering a Culture of Appreciation and Recognition

Appreciation is not just a one-time event but an ongoing commitment to valuing the faculty, demonstrating admiration, and expressing gratitude consistently. Just as in personal relationships, consistent appreciation is key to nurturing trust, respect, and open communication with teachers and staff.

To emphasize the importance of this culture change, consider the Gallup survey which asked more than 25 million employees around the world, including more than 100,000 educators, about what makes them engaged at work. K-12 teachers rated one item lower than any other on the survey: "In the last seven days, I have received recognition or praise for doing good work." Shockingly, only 29% of teachers in Gallup's survey "strongly agree" with this statement (source: Gallup's *State of America's Schools* report).

This data underscores the critical need for a culture of appreciation within the educational system. Being recognized not only makes teachers feel good but also improves their perception of school leaders. In the same survey, Gallup asked teachers to rate their principals on various measures, including management style, philosophy, and school climate.

Effective principals, as rated by their teachers, engage in these appreciative behaviors:

◆ **Value Recognition as a Frequent and Ongoing Activity:** They consider recognition a vital part of building a strong, positive school culture.

◆ **See Recognition as a Key Driver of Success:** They recognize that it's not just another event on their calendar but a fundamental element of school success.

◆ **Take a Hands-On Approach:** These principals actively participate in the recognition process, personally getting involved.

◆ **Encourage a Culture of Recognition:** They don't limit recognition to themselves; instead, they create an environment where everyone plays a role in appreciating one another.

As the research clearly indicates, the current culture needs to change. By creating a new culture of appreciation, you not only positively impact your faculty but also significantly enhance how your faculty views you as a leader. It's a win-win situation, fostering a more positive and productive educational environment for everyone involved.

To effectively demonstrate appreciation, it's crucial to consider both the words and actions that convey it. The following strategies, which align with the feedback gathered from surveys of teachers, reflect the most common responses on how administrators can show more appreciation:

◆ **Be Clear and Consistent:** Transparency is vital in fostering trust. School leaders should not hesitate to admit their mistakes and take responsibility for them. Consistency in their actions and decisions helps build a sense of reliability.

◆ **Value Communication and Listening:** Teachers appreciate when their voices are heard and their input is respected. Effective communication involves not only conveying information but also actively listening to the concerns, suggestions, and ideas of teachers. It's important to create an environment where teachers feel that their opinions are valued and considered.

◆ **Build Relationships:** Genuine appreciation is often rooted in meaningful relationships. School leaders can strengthen their connections with teachers by being more visible in the school community. Conducting classroom walkthroughs and visits not only shows interest but also provides valuable opportunities for engagement.

◆ **Avoid Favoritism:** Recognizing and appreciating all teachers, rather than just favorites, is crucial. Fairness and equity in appreciation efforts ensure that all staff members feel valued and motivated.

◆ **Involve Teachers in Decision-Making:** Empowering teachers by involving them in decision-making processes is a powerful way to show respect for their expertise and opinions. This collaborative approach reinforces a culture of appreciation.

◆ **Balance Workload and Acknowledge Existing Contributions:** Recognizing the efforts teachers are already putting in and avoiding overloading them with additional tasks or responsibilities is essential. Acknowledging their existing contributions is a form of appreciation. As one teacher expressed, "Stop adding more to our plate and provide more acknowledgment of what we already do."

◆ **Publicly Acknowledge Teaching:** Acknowledge and celebrate teachers' innovative teaching methods or out-standing efforts during staff meetings or school assemblies. For instance, commend a teacher for their creative use of technology to engage students in a difficult subject, showcasing how their initiative positively impacted the classroom learning experience. This not only highlights their achievements but also inspires others to explore new teaching approaches.

These strategies can be categorized into two overarching themes: relationships and character traits, such as respect and trust.

Building a culture of appreciation involves both connecting with teachers on a personal level and demonstrating these traits consistently. While some of these strategies will be discussed in more detail in later chapters, it's important to connect them with appreciation and recognition here to lay the foundation for a culture of appreciation within the educational institution.

As the research shows, everyone needs to be appreciated and recognized for their contributions. Therefore, when considering appreciation, it's crucial to extend it to all staff members in the educational institution. This includes custodians, bus drivers, lunchroom workers, and office staff. Visitors to the school can sense the leadership's commitment to appreciation through how the staff and teachers greet and interact with them. Ultimately, creating a culture of appreciation is a two-way street. By appreciating and recognizing the efforts of all staff members, school leaders are likely to find themselves more appreciated for their own leadership efforts in return.

Empowering Autonomy

Empowering teachers and staff through decision-making and autonomy is not merely a strategic approach; it represents a profound declaration of trust and respect for their professionalism within the educational institution. In a field where educators often grapple with feelings of undervaluation and underappreciation, affording them a voice and a degree of autonomy can be transformative. It sends an unequivocal message that their expertise is not just acknowledged but genuinely cherished.

This empowering philosophy finds a kindred spirit in the management style embodied by Lee Iacocca, as mentioned at the outset of this chapter. He astutely grasped the potency of granting employees autonomy and decision-making authority, a practice that not only ignited motivation among his workforce but also sparked a revolution in the automotive industry. Iacocca's approach compellingly illustrates that there is no more powerful way to convey appreciation for professionals than by entrusting them with the responsibility of making critical decisions.

Translating this concept into the realm of education, school leaders can draw inspiration from Iacocca's approach. By delegating decision-making authority to educators, they demonstrate unwavering confidence in their capabilities and a deep commitment to their profession. This empowerment extends across various facets of the educational process. It encompasses the freedom to choose teaching methods and materials that best align with students' needs, as well as participation in decisions concerning curriculum development and classroom policies.

Three major strategies to implement this empowerment effectively are:

1. **Collaborative Curriculum Development**
   - **Strategy:** Involve teachers in the decision-making process for curriculum development and improvement. Allow them to have a say in selecting teaching materials, designing lesson plans, and identifying learning objectives.
   - **Example:** Teachers in a middle school are given the opportunity to participate in curriculum committees where they provide input on the selection of textbooks, development of interdisciplinary projects, and alignment of curriculum with state standards. This collaborative approach ensures that the curriculum is tailored to meet the unique needs of their students.
2. **Professional Development Choices**
   - **Strategy:** Offer teachers autonomy in choosing their professional development opportunities. Allow them to identify areas for growth and select workshops, training, or courses that align with their interests and career goals.
   - **Example:** A high school allows teachers to create individualized professional development plans. Teachers can choose from a menu of options, such as attending conferences, pursuing advanced degrees, or participating in online courses. This autonomy

enables teachers to stay current in their field and develop expertise in areas that matter most to them and their students.

3. **Shared Decision-Making Committees**
   - **Strategy:** Establish committees or councils composed of teachers and staff to collaboratively make decisions on school policies, procedures, and practices. Encourage open dialogue and active participation in shaping the school's culture and environment.
   - **Example:** A school forms a School Improvement Team consisting of teachers, administrators, parents, and community members. This team meets regularly to discuss and make decisions on matters such as school discipline policies, extracurricular activities, and school culture initiatives. Teachers on the team have an equal voice in shaping the direction of the school and its policies.

When educators are vested with influence in these vital matters, they cultivate a profound sense of ownership and responsibility. This newfound autonomy propels them toward innovation and fosters a proactive approach in their professional roles. As a result, educators become more deeply invested in their work, and this enthusiasm directly benefits students. Motivated educators are more inclined to engage in innovative teaching practices, adapt to emerging pedagogical approaches, and remain informed about the latest trends in educational research.

In summary, empowering teachers and staff through decision-making and autonomy serves not only as a motivational strategy but also as a profound affirmation of their worth and professionalism. It nurtures a sense of ownership, amplifies job satisfaction, and bolsters the commitment to achieving student success. When educators experience such empowerment, they are more inclined to innovate, seize initiative, and contribute positively to the overarching growth and enhancement of the educational institution. This empowerment not only enriches the lives of educators but also forges a favorable and dynamic educational milieu where students can flourish.

Leadership Edge: Empowering, Understanding, and Appreciating Educators

Empowering and motivating teachers and staff is fundamental to successful educational leadership. It involves fostering a sense of ownership, responsibility, and commitment among educators, leading to proactive engagement and collaborative learning environments. Such a leadership approach not only enhances teacher job satisfaction but also directly benefits students through innovative teaching practices and personalized support. School leaders who prioritize teacher empowerment and motivation gain a competitive edge by creating a harmonious and productive educational community where students thrive, academic outcomes improve, and educators feel valued and inspired.

Understanding the unique needs and challenges of teachers and staff is another crucial aspect of effective leadership. By actively engaging in one-on-one interactions, conducting aspirational conversations, and seeking input through surveys and decision-making involvement, leaders build trust and open dialogue within the school community. This understanding enables leaders to provide tailored support and demonstrate their commitment to educators' professional growth. School leaders who take these steps gain a competitive edge by nurturing a positive work environment that attracts and retains talented educators, ensuring stability and consistency in the teaching staff, and, in turn, enhancing the overall educational experience.

Furthermore, fostering a culture of appreciation and recognition is a strategic imperative for school leaders. Consistently recognizing educators' efforts and involving them in decision-making processes not only boosts teacher morale but also positively shapes their perception of school leadership. Leaders who prioritize this culture change gain a competitive edge by creating a more positive and productive educational environment. Ultimately, school leaders who empower and motivate their teachers and staff, understand their unique needs, and foster a culture of appreciation, position themselves as effective leaders who drive success and continuous improvement within their educational institutions.

Enhancing Teacher Morale and Job Satisfaction through Compassion

It's important to note that teachers often exhibit high levels of agreeableness and a need for affirmation. This characteristic is significant when considering compassionate leadership as a means to enhance teacher morale and job satisfaction.

Teachers with high levels of agreeableness tend to be more cooperative, empathetic, and eager to please. They thrive in environments where they feel supported and valued. Compassionate leadership aligns perfectly with these traits, as it emphasizes empathy, understanding, and acknowledgment of teachers' efforts.

When compassionate leaders express appreciation and gratitude for their teachers' hard work, it resonates particularly well with those high in agreeableness. These teachers are more likely to respond positively to such gestures and, in turn, experience a boost in morale and job satisfaction.

Moreover, teachers who need affirmation benefit greatly from compassionate leadership. Compassionate leaders not only acknowledge their efforts but also actively listen to their concerns. This type of support provides the affirmation and validation that these teachers seek. They feel heard, valued, and appreciated, which enhances their overall job satisfaction and motivation.

The compatibility between compassionate leadership and the agreeableness and need for affirmation often found in teachers makes it a powerful approach for enhancing teacher morale and job satisfaction. Compassionate leaders create an environment where teachers can thrive, feel valued, and ultimately contribute to a positive and productive learning environment.

9

Relationship-Centered Leadership

The Foundation of Educational Success

On a sunny day in Chicago, I found myself at the base of the Willis Tower, ready to embark on a journey that would take me to the Skydeck at the top of the tower, which may be the highest viewing platform in the world. Even though I was in town to speak at multiple schools, I couldn't resist the opportunity to visit this iconic skyscraper. Little did I know that this visit would reveal a powerful lesson about relationships as the foundation for achieving vision and purpose, much like a building rising into the sky.

As I stepped into the lobby, the enormity of the tower surrounded me, and I marveled at the engineering feat before me. I approached the elevator, eager to ascend to the tower's dizzying heights. But to my surprise, the journey began by descending two stories below the bustling streets of Chicago.

It struck me as an unusual start – going down before going up. Yet, as I descended, I couldn't help but think of the foundations of the Willis Tower, reaching what I learned later was an astounding 100 feet into the earth, all the way to the bedrock beneath.

DOI: 10.4324/9781032657745-10

As the elevator began to rise, the walls displayed images of iconic structures around the world, including the Eiffel Tower, the Colosseum, the Statue of Liberty, and the Empire State Building. Despite their diverse designs and purposes, they all shared one crucial feature: a strong foundation.

These structures' diversity served as a vivid reminder that while appearances and purposes may differ, a strong and unwavering foundation is essential. Just as these remarkable buildings needed such foundations to reach their full potential and rise to awe-inspiring heights, school leaders require a similarly strong foundation of relationships to elevate their educational institutions to greatness.

This lesson underscores that while the visions or purposes of schools may take on different forms, the foundational need for strong relationships remains a constant. School leaders must understand that regardless of their specific educational mission, they share a common need for relationships as the cornerstone upon which to build a culture of excellence, collaboration, and shared purpose. It's the unshakable foundation that enables them to reach for the sky in their pursuit of educational greatness.

Consider the importance of relationships in the daily life of a school. A principal who has established strong connections with their teaching staff is better equipped to lead, inspire, and guide those educators toward a shared vision of academic excellence. Similarly, teachers who foster positive relationships with their students create an environment where learning thrives, as students feel valued and motivated to excel.

Moreover, the network of relationships extends beyond the school walls. Effective educational leaders build bridges with parents, community members, and other stakeholders. These relationships strengthen the entire educational ecosystem, fostering a sense of collective responsibility and shared commitment to the success of students.

In essence, while relationships may not always be the most apparent aspect or need of educational leadership, they are undeniably the most crucial. Just as the Willis Tower's grandeur relies on its hidden foundation, the success and endurance of educational institutions depend on the strength and depth of the relationships they cultivate. Without these deep and meaningful connections, leadership in education would be like a towering structure without a foundation – unsustainable, fragile, and destined to crumble under the weight of its challenges. It's a lesson that highlights the vital role of relationships in shaping the present and future of educational leadership.

Leadership Is Relationship-Centered

I have consistently emphasized the pivotal role of relationships in education. In the realm of education, which is inherently people-oriented, relationships must serve as the very foundation for its success. While we recognize the importance of fostering connections in the classroom, particularly between teachers and students, this critical aspect often seems to be disregarded when it comes to interactions among adults. However, I firmly maintain that leadership and the essence of education are fundamentally built on relationships. Genuine connections are where trust is not only established but also thrives, transcending mere transactional interactions among school leaders, teachers, and staff. These relationships form the bedrock of a positive school culture, enabling effective collaboration, problem-solving, and improved student outcomes. In fact, we have coined the term "interrelational leadership" to describe the leadership style that is not only most needed but potentially the most effective in education.

So, when I assert the importance of interrelational leadership, it's important to recognize that these relationships within the educational realm encompass far more than mere emotions and feelings; they represent the backbone of a dynamic and purposeful partnership. Within this collaborative framework, educators, administrators, and stakeholders converge, forging a unified front to navigate the educational landscape and work cohesively towards common goals and objectives. Their collective efforts are driven by an unwavering dedication to the overarching purpose of education – the holistic growth and development of every student.

These educational relationships rise above individual sentiments and superficial connections. They embody a robust and productive synergy, deeply rooted in mutual support, encouragement, and an unwavering commitment to excellence. This commitment extends not only to academic success but also to the personal growth and well-being of every student. It fosters an inclusive environment where diverse learners can thrive, nurturing their intellectual curiosity, social skills, and emotional resilience, ultimately preparing them to excel in a rapidly evolving world. When you think of it from this perspective, you can't help but see that it is the foundation for a successful, culture, team, and school.

The Key Principles of Relationship-Centered Leadership

Relationship-centered leadership is built on a foundation of key principles that guide leaders in their interactions and decision-making. These principles serve as a roadmap for cultivating strong relationships and creating a positive and inclusive school culture. Let's explore some of these essential principles:

1. **Trust:** Trust is critical to the success of any relationship. Relationship-centered leaders prioritize open and honest communication, ensuring that all members of the educational community feel heard, respected, and included. By fostering an environment of trust and transparency, leaders can create a sense of psychological safety, where individuals feel comfortable taking risks, sharing ideas, and engaging in meaningful dialogue.
   - *Alignment with Vision*: Trust in the unwavering commitment of school leadership to its vision is essential, as it unites everyone toward a shared goal of excellence and cultivates a sense of unity and purpose. In an environment characterized by strong and positive relationships, rallying individuals around a common vision becomes more seamless and effective. Teachers are more inclined to wholeheartedly adopt the vision when they have confidence in leadership's dedication to making it a reality, ultimately fostering a more robust and tightly-knit educational community.

- *Commitment to Purpose*: Trust fosters teachers' commitment to a shared mission, making them integral contributors who go above and beyond for their students, fueling their passion for teaching. In an environment of trust, educators are more willing to invest their time and energy in pursuit of the school's mission. This commitment to purpose is amplified when relationships are positive, as teachers feel valued and supported, driving them to excel in their roles.
- *Motivation and Engagement*: Trust motivates teachers, making them feel valued and committed to student success, resulting in enhanced classroom enthusiasm and an inspiring learning environment. When educators trust their colleagues and leaders, they are more motivated to give their best in the classroom. This heightened motivation translates into increased student engagement and a dynamic, enriching educational experience.
- *Collaboration and Interdependence*: Trust encourages collaboration, enriching the educational experience through shared expertise and innovative approaches, ultimately benefiting all involved. Strong, positive relationships among staff members create an environment where collaboration is natural and productive. Teachers are more likely to share their ideas, resources, and best practices when trust prevails, leading to collective growth and improved outcomes for students.
- *Transparency and Communication*: Trust is linked to transparent and effective communication, building credibility and engagement by keeping stakeholders informed and involved in decision-making processes. Effective communication is vital in any educational institution, and trust is the foundation upon which it thrives. When relationships are strong and positive, open and honest communication becomes the norm, ensuring that all stakeholders are well-informed and feel heard, which in turn strengthens their commitment to the school's success. An example

would be a new school principal arriving at a school with a history of turnover in leadership. They take the time to meet individually with each staff member. During these meetings, they actively listen to staff concerns, acknowledge past challenges, and commit to transparency and open communication moving forward. This genuine effort to connect and empathize with the staff's previous experiences gradually earns their trust, leading to a more cohesive and motivated team.

2. **Empathy and Understanding:** Empathy and understanding stand as cornerstone attributes of relationship-centered leaders in education. These leaders possess a profound awareness of the individual needs, backgrounds, and perspectives of their team members. They go beyond the surface and actively engage in listening, seeking to truly comprehend the experiences and challenges that teachers and staff face.

   • One of the distinguishing traits of such leaders is their ability to put themselves in others' shoes, to feel what their team members are feeling, and to respond with genuine empathy. This empathy extends beyond superficial gestures; it is a heartfelt understanding of the emotions, struggles, and aspirations of those they lead.

   • In practical terms, relationship-centered leaders take the time to have meaningful conversations with their team members. They create spaces where teachers and staff feel safe sharing their thoughts, concerns, and ideas without fear of judgment. This open and empathetic communication fosters trust and a sense of belonging within the school community.

   • For example, A school principal may notice a teacher struggling with a challenging student. Instead of prescribing solutions, the principal actively listens to the teacher's concerns and offers support, demonstrating genuine empathy and understanding. This approach fosters trust, leading to improved teacher morale and ultimately better student outcomes.

- By demonstrating care and concern for the well-being of their educators and staff, these leaders create a supportive and compassionate environment. This atmosphere not only promotes emotional well-being but also encourages professional growth and success. Teachers and staff are more likely to be motivated and engaged when they know their leaders genuinely care about their happiness and development.
- When leaders exhibit empathy and understanding, they set a powerful example for their team. This can have a ripple effect throughout the organization, inspiring others to cultivate similar qualities of compassion, active listening, and genuine concern for their colleagues.

3. **Collaboration and Shared Decision-Making:** Collaboration and shared decision-making are vital components of relationship-centered leadership in education. These leaders recognize that building strong relationships goes hand in hand with involving their team members in the decision-making process. By doing so, they not only empower their staff but also harness the collective knowledge and expertise within the organization, leading to more innovative and effective solutions.

- In practice, relationship-centered leaders create an environment where collaboration is not just encouraged but actively supported. They seek input and feedback from their team members on a regular basis, whether it's regarding curriculum development, school policies, or strategies to address challenges. This involvement sends a clear message that every member of the team is valued and that their insights matter.
- Furthermore, these leaders ensure that the decision-making process is transparent and inclusive. They

communicate the rationale behind decisions and provide opportunities for open dialogue. This transparency helps build trust within the team, as everyone understands the reasons behind certain choices, even if they don't always agree with them.

Unlocking the Power of Strong Relationships in Education: A Path to Commitment and Success

Benefits of strong relationships in education extend far beyond the individual level, significantly impacting the entire school community. These relationships serve as the cornerstone of a school's culture, fostering a greater commitment to the institution's mission and purpose. In this exploration, we embark on a journey to uncover the profound advantages of cultivating robust connections within the educational landscape.

As we navigate through the following sections, we will delve deeper into these advantages, highlighting their pivotal role in strengthening the commitment to a school's overarching mission and purpose. From enhancing teacher engagement and student outcomes to nurturing a positive school culture and ensuring transparent communication of the school's mission, each facet of relationship-centered leadership contributes to a harmonious, productive, and mission-driven educational environment.

Join us as we unravel the interconnected web of relationships within education, recognizing their transformative power in elevating the commitment and success of all those engaged in the pursuit of educational excellence.

In essence, strong relationships in education create a ripple effect that extends from individual well-being to the collective commitment to the school's mission and purpose. They form the foundation upon which a thriving educational community is built, where teachers, students, and leaders work cohesively towards a shared goal of excellence and innovation, shaping a culture of curiosity and resilience.

Empowering Relationships Through Assertive and Compassionate Strategies

Building and nurturing robust relationships within an educational context is a nuanced task, requiring a thoughtful blend of assertive and compassionate strategies. These strategies are meticulously designed to cultivate collaboration, understanding, and a shared dedication to educational goals. In this section, we explore these dynamic approaches employed by relationship-centered leaders to forge meaningful connections with teachers and staff.

Our approach recognizes that relationships in education transcend mere emotions and feelings; they are the cornerstone of a purpose-driven partnership. Within this framework, educators, administrators, and stakeholders unite to steer education towards a common mission. These relationships are rooted in mutual support, unwavering dedication, and a shared commitment to creating an environment where every student can thrive academically and personally.

In the following sections, we delve into three assertive strategies empowering leaders to establish clear expectations, foster open communication, and navigate conflicts effectively. Additionally, we explore three compassionate strategies that emphasize recognition, mentorship, and holistic well-being as fundamental aspects of nurturing a supportive educational community. Together, these strategies pave the way not only for academic excellence but also for the holistic growth and well-being of all participants in the educational journey.

Assertive Strategies

1. **Active Listening and Feedback Sessions:** Imagine a school leader, Jane, who schedules monthly one-on-one meetings with her teachers and staff. During these sessions, she actively listens to their concerns, ideas, and feedback. Jane takes notes during these conversations to demonstrate her commitment to their input. For instance, if a teacher raises concerns about classroom resources,

Jane follows up promptly by initiating a discussion with the school board to address these needs. This proactive approach validates the voices of her team and creates a culture of open communication.

2. **Clear Expectations and Accountability:** Consider a scenario where a school principal, David, establishes clear expectations for teacher performance and behavior. These expectations are communicated transparently to all staff members. When a teacher, Sarah, falls below these standards in classroom management, David provides constructive feedback and offers resources for improvement. By consistently upholding these expectations and providing guidance, David ensures a productive working environment for the entire school.

3. **Conflict Resolution Protocols:** In a school, conflicts can arise among staff members. To address this, the school leadership has implemented clear and equitable conflict resolution protocols. When a dispute arises between two teachers, Mark and Lisa, these protocols are activated. A neutral mediator facilitates the conversation, ensuring that both Mark and Lisa have the opportunity to voice their concerns respectfully. Through this structured and professional approach, the conflict is resolved, and a harmonious working relationship is reestablished.

Compassionate Strategies

1. **Recognition and Appreciation:** Picture a school where the principal, Emily, places a strong emphasis on recognizing and appreciating her staff. When a teacher, John, goes the extra mile to support a struggling student, Emily publicly acknowledges his efforts during a staff meeting. This heartfelt recognition not only boosts John's morale but also encourages others to take similar initiatives, fostering a sense of value and belonging within the school community.

2. **Supportive Mentoring:** In a school, experienced educators are encouraged to serve as mentors to newer colleagues.

Sarah, a veteran teacher, takes on the role of mentor to a new teacher, Alex. Beyond professional development, Sarah provides emotional support and guidance to help Alex navigate the challenges of the teaching profession. This mentorship not only enhances Alex's confidence but also strengthens the camaraderie among colleagues.

3. **Well-Being Check-Ins:** Regularly check in on the emotional and mental well-being of teachers and staff. Create an environment where they feel comfortable discussing stressors, and provide resources to manage workload and stress, demonstrating genuine care for their overall well-being. As a school leader, I would take time every morning to check in with each teacher individually to see how they're doing.

Challenges in Building and Maintaining Strong Relationships

Building and sustaining strong relationships within an educational community is the cornerstone of effective leadership and a thriving school environment. However, like any human endeavor, it comes with its share of challenges. Educational leaders must be adept at identifying and addressing these challenges to ensure that relationships remain robust and productive.

As we finish this chapter, let's delve into some of the common challenges faced by educational leaders in nurturing relationships, and offer practical solutions to overcome them. By acknowledging these challenges and implementing proactive strategies, leaders can foster a more cohesive and supportive educational community, ultimately benefiting teachers, staff, students, and parents alike.

1. Teacher Turnover
Challenge: High teacher turnover rates can disrupt the continuity of relationships within a school. Frequent departures make it challenging to establish lasting bonds with school leadership and colleagues.

Solution:

◆ *Implement Comprehensive Onboarding Programs:* Help new teachers quickly integrate into the school community by providing comprehensive onboarding programs that familiarize them with the school's culture, policies, and expectations.

◆ *Create Mentorship Initiatives:* Pair new teachers with experienced educators who can provide support and guidance during the critical initial phase of their career.

◆ *Conduct Exit Interviews:* Gain insights into the reasons for teacher departures by conducting exit interviews. Use this feedback to inform strategies aimed at improving teacher retention.

2. Communication Breakdowns

Challenge: Effective communication is vital for strong relationships, yet breakdowns can lead to misunderstandings, conflicts, and a lack of trust among staff members and between educators and leaders.

Solution:

◆ *Foster a Culture of Open Communication:* Encourage a culture of open and transparent communication within the school. Facilitate regular meetings, both formal and informal, where teachers, staff, and leaders can freely share ideas, concerns, and updates.

◆ *Utilize Various Communication Tools:* Employ a variety of communication tools and platforms, including digital channels, to ensure that information flows smoothly and is accessible to all stakeholders.

◆ *Provide Communication Training:* Offer communication training or workshops for educators and leaders to enhance their interpersonal and communication skills.

3. Resistance to Change

Challenge: The introduction of new initiatives, policies, or educational approaches can sometimes be met with resistance from staff members, straining relationships and hindering progress.

Solution:

- ◆ *Involve Teachers and Staff in Decision-Making:* Include teachers and staff in the decision-making process when implementing changes. Seek their input, actively listen to their concerns, and consider their suggestions.
- ◆ *Clearly Communicate Reasons for Change:* Clearly communicate the reasons behind changes and how they align with the school's mission and goals. Provide a compelling rationale for the proposed changes.
- ◆ *Offer Professional Development:* Equip educators with the skills and knowledge needed to navigate and embrace change successfully through professional development opportunities.

4. Conflict Resolution

Challenge: Conflicts inevitably arise in educational institutions and, if left unresolved, can damage relationships and create a hostile work environment.

Solution:

- ◆ *Establish Clear Conflict Resolution Protocols:* Set up clear and fair conflict resolution protocols within the school. Ensure that all parties involved understand the process for addressing disputes and conflicts.
- ◆ *Appoint Trained Mediators:* Appoint trained mediators or conflict resolution facilitators who can mediate conflicts and guide discussions toward resolution in a neutral and unbiased manner.
- ◆ *Cultivate a Culture of Forgiveness and Reconciliation:* Encourage a culture of forgiveness and reconciliation within the school community, where individuals are willing to put aside differences and work collaboratively towards common goals.

5. Parent–Teacher Relationships:

Challenge: Building and maintaining strong relationships with parents is essential for student success. However, differing expectations, communication challenges, or cultural differences can create hurdles.

Solution:

◆ *Organize Regular Parent–Teacher Meetings:* Establish regular parent–teacher conferences or meetings to establish a channel for dialogue and collaboration between educators and parents.

◆ *Provide Parent Resources and Workshops:* Offer resources and workshops for parents to help them understand the educational process and their role in supporting their child's learning.

◆ *Foster an Inclusive School Environment:* Create a welcoming and inclusive school environment that celebrates diversity and acknowledges the unique needs and perspectives of all parents.

By actively addressing these challenges and implementing thoughtful solutions, educational leaders can navigate the complexities of building and maintaining strong relationships, ultimately contributing to a more cohesive and supportive educational community where all stakeholders thrive.

Gaining the Edge: The Power of Relationships

Beneath the towering presence of the Willis Tower, where architectural wonders reach skyward, we've learned a vital lesson about education – relationships are its foundation. Like the solid foundations supporting these grand structures, relationships underpin the excellence of educational institutions.

In leadership and education, relationships take center stage. Think about the principal who fosters strong connections with their teaching staff, enabling better leadership, inspiration, and guidance. Consider the teacher who builds positive relationships with students, creating an environment where learning thrives through a sense of value and motivation to excel.

These networks of relationships extend beyond school walls. Effective educational leaders establish connections with parents, community members, and stakeholders, strengthening the educational ecosystem and fostering collective responsibility for student success.

Relationships may not always be the most visible aspect of educational leadership, but they are undeniably the most crucial. Just as the grandeur of the Willis Tower relies on its hidden foundation, the success and endurance of educational institutions depend on the strength and depth of the relationships they cultivate. Without these meaningful connections, leadership in education would be like a towering structure without a foundation – unsustainable and fragile, destined to crumble under its challenges.

Moreover, it's essential to recognize that relationships give a leader a distinct competitive edge in being an effective leader. Leaders who prioritize building strong connections with their staff, students, parents, and the community create a more cohesive and harmonious educational environment. This trust and rapport foster open communication, collaboration, and a shared commitment to the institution's goals.

For instance, a principal who maintains positive relationships with their teaching staff is more likely to inspire and motivate educators to excel in their roles. This, in turn, leads to improved teaching quality, student engagement, and overall academic outcomes. Likewise, teachers who establish meaningful connections with their students create a classroom atmosphere where students feel valued, safe, and motivated to learn.

Furthermore, leaders who extend their relationships beyond the school's boundaries by engaging with parents, community members, and stakeholders build a network of support that can enhance the school's resources, reputation, and opportunities for growth. This community involvement not only strengthens the school's position but also demonstrates leadership's commitment to a holistic educational experience.

Relationships are not only the foundation of education but also a critical asset for effective leadership. They empower leaders to inspire and guide their teams, motivate students, and engage with the broader community. Leaders who understand the significance of relationships and prioritize cultivating them gain a competitive edge in driving success and enduring excellence within their educational institutions. Just as the Willis Tower stands tall due to its hidden foundation, leaders with strong relationships create enduring, successful educational environments.

10

Maximizing Your Leadership Edge

A school leader's path to success is marked by two essential elements: achieving important goals and fulfilling a mission driven by a clear sense of purpose. These goals serve as guiding points, providing direction and motivation in the journey. To achieve them, assertiveness plays a crucial role – a steadfast commitment to setting and achieving high standards, especially when challenges arise. Goals and purpose act as strong foundations upon which leaders build their vision for the future.

However, effective school leadership goes beyond merely reaching these goals. It equally emphasizes compassion – an authentic understanding and empathy for the unique needs, strengths, and challenges of the individuals they lead. At its core, leadership is about guiding people toward growth and success, all grounded in a sense of purpose. Empathy, the ability to connect with others on a deeply human level, empowers leaders to provide genuine support, encouragement, and build strong relationships.

In essence, successful school leadership is a delicate balance – a harmonious interplay between pursuing goals, nurturing empathy, and remaining steadfast in one's sense of purpose. All three components are essential. Goals provide direction, empathy fosters trust and cohesion among leaders and their teams, and a clear sense of purpose anchors the entire endeavor.

To maximize their leadership edge and become a highly effective leader, school leaders must recognize and embrace

DOI: 10.4324/9781032657745-11

this profound balance. It serves as the cornerstone for personal and collective growth, forming the basis for an inclusive, innovative, and thriving educational environment. The strong relationships that flourish within this equilibrium between assertiveness, empathy, and purpose become the bedrock of exceptional educational leadership, ultimately paving the way to educational success.

The Power of Purpose

The power of purpose in educational leadership is like a compass guiding the way for school leaders and their teams. It's not just a concept but the key to uniting everyone towards a common goal. Purpose is what unifies school leaders, teachers, and students, and its importance cannot be overstated.

- ◆ **Defining Your Leadership Purpose:** Defining your leadership purpose is like creating a roadmap for your journey as an educational leader. It involves introspection and self-discovery. Start by asking yourself essential questions: Why did you choose a career in education leadership? What are your long-term aspirations for your school or district? What positive changes do you hope to bring about? Reflecting on your experiences and identifying moments of fulfillment or impact can help you pinpoint your purpose. Perhaps you find deep satisfaction in mentoring teachers or in creating an inclusive school culture. Your purpose may revolve around empowering students to reach their full potential or advocating for equitable educational opportunities. As you uncover your purpose, it becomes a source of inspiration and motivation, guiding your decisions and actions as a leader.
- ◆ **Inspiring Others:** Once you've defined your leadership purpose, the next step is to inspire and motivate others, including your colleagues, staff, and students. Effective leadership involves sharing your purpose with passion and authenticity. Communicate your vision and mission

clearly, explaining how they align with the broader goals of education. Share personal anecdotes or stories of leaders who have inspired you. By demonstrating unwavering dedication to your purpose and consistently modeling the values and principles you hold dear, you become a source of inspiration to those around you. As a leader, you have the opportunity to create a sense of purpose and direction within your educational community, motivating others to join you in the pursuit of shared goals. Leading with purpose not only fosters enthusiasm and commitment but also fosters a culture of trust and collaboration, where everyone is aligned toward a common objective.

◆ **Leading with Values:** Leading with values is about anchoring your leadership approach in a set of core principles that guide your actions and decisions. Values are the compass that keeps you on course, especially when facing challenges or difficult choices. To lead with values, first, identify your core principles and beliefs as a leader. These could include integrity, equity, accountability, or innovation. Then, consistently demonstrate these values in your leadership style. Uphold them even when confronted with adversity, showcasing your commitment to your purpose and the values that underpin it. Leading with values not only creates a strong ethical foundation for your leadership but also sets a clear example for your team and your educational community. When values are shared and embraced, they create a sense of unity and purpose that can drive positive change and lead to a thriving educational environment.

Developing Your Leadership Skills: Nurturing Your Strengths for Effective Leadership

The journey of leadership development is a dynamic and multifaceted process that requires continuous self-discovery, growth, and a keen focus on individual strengths. Effective leadership hinges on recognizing and nurturing these strengths to maximize their positive impact within educational institutions. This strategy underscores the importance of aligning leadership skills with personal strengths to become an influential and impactful educational leader.

◆ **Strengths Assessment and Self-Reflection:** The foundational step in nurturing your strengths for effective leadership is self-awareness. Leaders should engage in strengths assessments and self-reflection exercises to identify and understand their unique talents, values, and motivations. Tools like a Big Five Personality Assessment or the CliftonStrengths assessment can provide valuable insights into one's strengths and personality traits. This self-discovery process empowers leaders to leverage their innate abilities effectively.

 Example: *An educational leader, after taking the CliftonStrengths assessment, discovers that their top strengths include "communication" and "strategic thinking." They reflect on how these strengths have contributed to their success and formulate strategies to incorporate them into their leadership style.*

◆ **Strengths-Based Leadership Development Plans:** Once leaders have identified their strengths, they should create personalized leadership development plans centered on nurturing and utilizing these strengths. These plans outline specific actions, goals, and milestones for enhancing leadership skills in alignment with individual strengths. Leaders may seek mentorship or coaching to refine their strengths and leverage them strategically.

 Example: *A school principal with a strength in "empathy" creates a leadership development plan that includes activities like empathetic listening workshops, mentoring sessions, and peer feedback mechanisms to further develop their empathetic leadership style.*

◆ **Collaborative Leadership Teams:** Fostering collaborative leadership teams that encompass a diverse range of strengths is a strategic approach. Educational leaders should assemble teams with complementary strengths to address multifaceted challenges. This diversity of strengths within the leadership team ensures a balanced and holistic approach to problem-solving and decision-making.

Example: *A superintendent forms an executive leadership team where each member possesses distinct strengths such as "analytical thinking," "relationship-building," and "innovation." Together, they leverage their strengths to tackle complex issues, create innovative solutions, and nurture a collaborative leadership culture throughout the district.*

◆ **Strengths-Based Coaching and Mentoring:** Leaders benefit from coaching and mentoring relationships that focus on strengths-based development. Seasoned educational leaders or executive coaches can provide guidance and insights to help individuals harness their strengths effectively. These mentors can offer constructive feedback, share experiences, and encourage leaders to apply their strengths in real-world scenarios.

Example: *A new assistant principal seeks a mentor with a strong background in educational leadership. Through regular coaching sessions, the mentor identifies the assistant principal's strengths and guides them in using these strengths to build positive relationships with teachers, resulting in improved staff morale.*

◆ **Ongoing Growth and Adaptation:** Leadership development is an ongoing journey that demands adaptability and a commitment to continuous growth. Leaders should embrace opportunities for professional development, attend relevant workshops and conferences, and stay informed about emerging trends in education. This dedication to learning ensures that leaders remain agile and responsive in their leadership roles.

Example: *A school district superintendent dedicates time each year to attend national conferences on educational leadership. This commitment to ongoing growth exposes them to innovative ideas, best practices, and the latest research, allowing them to adapt their leadership strategies to meet evolving educational challenges.*

In essence, nurturing your strengths for effective leadership involves a holistic approach to leadership development. It begins with self-awareness, extends to personalized leadership plans, incorporates collaborative teamwork, leverages coaching and mentoring, and embraces a commitment to continuous growth. By aligning leadership skills with individual strengths, educational leaders can not only maximize their effectiveness but also create a positive and thriving environment within their institutions.

Balancing Leadership with Self-Care: Sustaining Your Leadership Edge

While maximizing your leadership edge is essential for success in the educational landscape, it's equally important to recognize the significance of self-care in sustaining your leadership journey. Educational leadership can be demanding, and the responsibilities can be overwhelming at times. To maintain your effectiveness and well-being, it's crucial to incorporate self-care practices into your leadership approach.

◆ **Prioritizing Well-Being:** The cornerstone of effective leadership is personal well-being. Prioritizing your physical, emotional, and mental health is not a luxury but a necessity. Leaders who neglect self-care risk burnout and diminished performance. Dedicate time to exercise, maintain a balanced diet, and get adequate sleep. Engage in relaxation techniques such as meditation or mindfulness to manage stress. By taking care of yourself, you'll have the energy and resilience needed to navigate the challenges of educational leadership.

   Example: *A school principal allocates time each morning for a brief meditation session before starting the day. This practice helps them remain calm and focused, even during high-pressure situations.*

◆ **Setting Boundaries:** Educational leaders often face the temptation to work long hours, extending well beyond the typical school day. While dedication is commendable, setting clear boundaries is crucial. Establish limits on work hours and refrain from bringing work-related stress home. Communicate these boundaries to your team and colleagues to foster a culture of work–life balance.

Example: *A district superintendent designates specific "unplugged" evenings during the week to spend quality time with their family, ensuring a healthy work–life balance.*

♦ **Delegating Responsibility:** Effective leadership involves delegation. Recognize that you don't need to shoulder every responsibility alone. Delegate tasks and responsibilities to capable team members, trusting their abilities. Delegation not only lightens your workload but also empowers others to develop their leadership skills.

Example: *An assistant principal delegates certain administrative tasks to department heads, allowing them to take ownership of their areas and contribute to the school's success.*

♦ **Seeking Support and Connection:** Leadership can be isolating, but it doesn't have to be. Seek support from mentors, peers, or support groups for educational leaders. Sharing experiences and challenges with others who understand your role can provide valuable insights and emotional support.

Example: *A school principal participates in a monthly leadership roundtable with other principals from neighboring schools. These gatherings allow them to exchange ideas, vent frustrations, and offer mutual support.*

♦ **Celebrating Achievements:** Don't forget to celebrate your achievements, both big and small. Acknowledge your successes and milestones, and share these moments with your team. Celebrations create a positive and motivating atmosphere within your educational community.

Example: *A school superintendent hosts a quarterly "Success Showcase" where exceptional accomplishments of teachers, students, and staff are celebrated. This practice boosts morale and fosters a sense of achievement.*

Incorporating self-care practices into your leadership approach isn't a sign of weakness; it's a sign of wisdom. It allows you to sustain your leadership edge, ensuring that you remain resilient, focused, and compassionate in your role. Remember that effective leadership isn't about burning out but about leading with vitality, purpose, and a commitment to both your well-being and the success of your educational community. Balancing your leadership with self-care not only benefits you but also sets a positive example for your team and fosters a culture of well-being and resilience within your institution.

Strategies for Maximizing Your Leadership Edge

Ideally you have learned many important strategies to help you balance your leadership approach. It's important to remember that to be a successful school leader, you have to adopt a proactive approach, continuously refine your leadership skills, and stay attuned to the evolving needs of your educational community.

◆ **Embrace Innovation:** World-class school leadership hinges on wholeheartedly embracing innovation. In today's ever-evolving educational landscape, leaders wield the power to drive positive change by daring to innovate. Cultivate a culture of innovation within your school, encouraging staff members to experiment with new teaching methods, technologies, and approaches. Such an environment not only fosters enhanced learning outcomes but also infuses the school with a more vibrant culture, ultimately benefiting both students and educators.

◆ **Self-Reflection:** Self-reflection is a cornerstone of effective leadership. Take the time to introspect and evaluate your actions, decisions, and leadership style. Understand your strengths and areas for improvement. Through self-reflection you gain deeper insights into your leadership approach and can make more informed decisions that benefit your school community.

◆ **Self-Improvement:** Leaders who continuously evolve through personal growth inspire their teams and set the stage for long-lasting success. Prioritizing self-improvement as an integral component of your leadership strategy is paramount. Invest in your own development, acquiring the skills and insights needed to lead with excellence. But remember your greatest success will come from maximizing your strengths, more than just focusing on perceived weaknesses. It's your unique strengths that give you an edge no one else possesses.

◆ **Foster Strategic Collaboration:** Effective school leaders should place strategic collaboration at the forefront of their leadership approach. Actively seek partnerships with other schools, educators, and community organizations to tap into a wealth of resources, ideas, and support. Strategic collaboration harnesses the collective knowledge and expertise of various stakeholders, fostering synergy that can lead to innovative solutions to complex challenges. Collaborative efforts can yield shared professional development opportunities, collaborative research projects, and the exchange of best practices. Furthermore, it can enhance your school's visibility and reputation within the broader educational community.

◆ **Empower and Inspire:** World-class leaders empower and inspire their teams to reach new heights. Encourage autonomy and creativity among your educators and staff. Provide opportunities for them to take ownership of their roles and projects, fostering a sense of ownership and pride in their work. By instilling a shared vision and purpose, you inspire a collective commitment to achieving educational excellence.

◆ **Emphasize Strong Relationships with Teachers:** Building strong and positive relationships with teachers is foundational to effective school leadership. Establish open lines of communication and trust with your teaching staff. Regularly meet with them to understand their ideas, concerns, and aspirations. Create a supportive environment where they feel valued and motivated to contribute to the school's success. Nurturing these relationships not only enhances teamwork but also ensures that everyone is aligned with the school's mission and goals, ultimately leading to a more harmonious and successful educational community.

These strategies, with a focus on relationships with teachers, provide a comprehensive framework for world-class leadership in education. They emphasize innovation, personal growth, collaboration, empowerment, and strong interpersonal connections, which are all crucial elements for navigating the complexities of the educational landscape and achieving excellence for students and educators.

As we wrap up our time together, I want to leave you with this thought; every leader, including you, has the potential to make a lasting impact on education. Whether you're a school principal, a district superintendent, or in any other educational role, you have the power to inspire students and staff to reach their fullest potential, to innovate in the face of challenges, and to leave behind a legacy of positive change.

Embrace your unique leadership journey, for it is in your distinct experiences, perspectives, and talents that you hold the key to unlocking a brighter future for education. Be a trailblazer, challenge the status quo, and champion the needs of your students, colleagues, and staff, as well as the broader community. By infusing your leadership with inspiration and empowerment, you not only elevate your own abilities but also ignite the spark of transformation in those you lead. Together, we can navigate the changing educational currents while staying true to both our principles and the pursuit of progress. The legacy you leave behind will serve as a testament to the lasting impact you've made not just on education, but on the lives of the people you've served.

Meet the Authors

Dr. Brad Johnson is one of the most dynamic and engaging speakers in the fields of education and leadership. He has 25 years of experience in the trenches as a teacher and administrator. Dr. Johnson is transforming how teachers lead in the classroom and how administrators lead in the school. He is a servant leader who shares his vast experience and expertise to help other educators maximize their potential. He is author of many books including *Dear Teacher* (with Hal Bowman), *Principal Bootcamp*, *Putting Teachers First*, and *Learning on Your Feet*. He has traveled the globe speaking and training teachers and educational leaders.

Jeremy Johnson earned a master's degree in Industrial/Organizational Psychology, where his research focused on the application of personality theory in the workplace. His extensive research and knowledge in the field have enabled him to gain a comprehensive understanding of human behavior in professional settings, making him an invaluable asset to any organization. He has 16 years experience, including a background in administrative processes and procedure development which has led to the implementation of streamlined workflows and improved efficiency in various projects. His exceptional leadership skills have also enabled him to develop and nurture the next generation of leaders within various organizations.

References

Ames, D., Lee, A., & Wazlawek, A. (2017). Interpersonal assertiveness: Inside the balancing act. *Social and Personality Psychology Compass*, 11(6).

Ames, D. R., & Flynn, F. J. (2007). What breaks a leader: The curvilinear relation between assertiveness and leadership. *Journal of Personality and Social Psychology*, 92(2), 307–324. https://doi.org/10.1037/0022-3514.92.2.307

Banks, R. (2020). *The keys to being brilliantly confident and more assertive: A vital guide to enhancing your communication skills, getting rid of anxiety, and building assertiveness*. Author.

Bolton, R. (2012). *People skills: How to assert yourself, listen to others, and resolve conflicts*. ReadHowYouWant.

Bradberry, T., & Greaves, J. (2009). *Emotional intelligence 2.0*. TalentSmart.

Chen, S.-C., Shao, J., Liu, N.-T., & Du, Y.-S. (2022). Reading the wind: Impacts of leader negative emotional expression on employee silence. *Frontiers in Psychology*, 13, 762920. https://doi.org/10.3389/fpsyg.2022.762920

Folkman, J. (2013, October 10). The 6 secrets of successfully assertive leaders. Forbes. Retrieved February 3, 2021, from https://www.forbes.com/sites/joefolkman/2013/10/10/the-6-secrets-of-successfully-assertive-leaders/?sh=2d8becd26668

Gallo, A. (2012, August 21). How to be assertive (without losing yourself). *Harvard Business Review*. Retrieved February 3, 2021, from https://hbr.org/2012/08/how-to-be-assertive-without-lo

Kuntze, J., Van der Molen, H. T., & Born, M. P. (2016). Big five personality traits and assertiveness do not affect mastery of communication skills. *Health Professions Education*, 2(1), 33–43. https://doi.org/10.1016/j.hpe.2016.01.009

Molinsky, A. (2017, August 31). A simple way to be more assertive (without being pushy). *Harvard Business Review*. Retrieved February 3, 2021, from https://hbr.org/2017/08/a-simple-way-to-be-more-assertive-without-being-pushy

Murphy, J. (2011). *Assertiveness: How to stand up for yourself and still win the respect of others*. Author.

Nevenglosky, E. A., Cale, C., & Aguilar, S. P. (2019). Barriers to effective curriculum implementation. *Research in Higher Education Journal*, Volume 36.

Pommier, E., Neff, K. D., & Tóth-Király, I. (2020). The development and validation of the Compassion Scale. *Assessment*, 27(1), 21–39. https://doi.org/10.1177/1073191119874108

Rosenthal, N. (2012, January 5). 10 Ways to Enhance Your Emotional Intelligence. *Psychology Today*.

Seco, V. M. M., & Lopes, M. P. (2014). Between compassionateness and assertiveness: A trust matrix for leaders. *Journal of Industrial Engineering and Management*, 7(3), 622–644. Online ISSN: 2014–0953. Print ISSN: 2014–8423. http://dx.doi.org/10.3926/jiem.1046

Wang, C.-H., Liu, G. H. W., & Lee, N. C.-A. (2021). Effects of passive leadership in the digital age. *Frontiers in Psychology*, 12, 701047. https://doi.org/10.3389/fpsyg.2021.701047

Made in the USA
Columbia, SC
04 June 2024

As a school leader, do you ever have trouble striking a balance between being agreeable and pleasing your staff, while also being assertive and making the hard decisions? In this empowering new book from Brad Johnson and Jeremy Johnson, you'll discover the tools and insights you need to fine-tune your leadership style and maximize your effectiveness while still building a great culture.

You'll learn how to find the balance between assertiveness and compassion that's right for you, allowing you to address challenges with confidence and empathy. You'll also explore the art of emotional intelligence and its role in building a harmonious school culture, where staff and students thrive. Each chapter is filled with practical strategies and examples to help you build your skills.

As you find your edge as a leader, you'll improve your results for the school and your relationships with staff, and you'll feel more fulfilled in your personal journey as well!

Brad Johnson is one of the most dynamic and engaging speakers in the fields of education and leadership. He has 25 years of experience in the trenches as a teacher and administrator. He is author of many books including *Dear Teacher* (with Hal Bowman), *Principal Bootcamp*, *Putting Teachers First*, and *Learning on Your Feet*. He has travelled the globe speaking and training teachers and educational leaders.

Jeremy Johnson earned a master's degree in Industrial/Organizational Psychology and has 16 years' experience, including a background in administrative processes and procedure development which has led to the implementation of streamlined workflows and improved efficiency in various projects. His exceptional leadership skills have also enabled him to develop and nurture the next generation of leaders within various organizations.

EDUCATION / LEADERSHIP

an **informa** business

ISBN 978-1-032-64407-3

Routledge
Taylor & Francis Group
www.routledge.com

CERTIFIED
CARBON
NEUTRAL
Publication
CarbonNeutral.com

Routledge titles are available as eBook editions in a range of digital formats